# Your First
# Business
# Plan

# Your First
# Business
# Plan 5TH EDITION

## A simple question-and-answer format designed to help you write your own plan

**Joseph Covello and Brian Hazelgren**

SOURCEBOOKS, INC.®
NAPERVILLE, ILLINOIS

This publication is designed to provide accurate and authoritative information in regard to
the subject matter covered. It is sold with the understanding that the publisher is not
engaged in rendering legal, accounting, or other professional service. If legal advice or other
expert assistance is required, the services of a competent professional person should be
sought. —From a Declaration of Principles Jointly Adopted by a Committee of the
American Bar Association and a Committee of Publishers and Associations

Published by: Sourcebooks, Inc.
P.O. Box 4410, Naperville, Illinois, 60567-4410
(630) 961-3900
Fax: (630) 961-2168
www.sourcebooks.com


Library of Congress Cataloging-in-Publication Data

Covello, Joseph A.
Your first business plan: a simple question and answer format designed to help you write a
plan / by Joseph Covello and Brian Hazelgren.—5th ed.
p. cm.Includes index.
ISBN 1-4022-0412-4
1. Business planning. 2. New business enterprises—Planning. 3. Small business—
Planning. I. Hazelgren, Brian J. II. Title.
   HD30.28 .C6967 2002
   658.4'012—dc21

                                                                    2002009773

Printed and bound in the United States of America
VP  20 19 18 17 16 15 14 13 12 11

# Contents

# Introduction

If you are a business owner, a business manager, or going into business for the first time, at some point you will need to develop a business plan. Whether you need to raise capital or create a clearer focus for your organization, a business plan is as necessary to the small business owner as a road map is to a traveler in new territory. The path to your final destination has a logical sequence, and a good road map will allow you to reach your goal with the smallest amount of hassle and frustration. This book explains the essential rules and strategies you will need to develop a simple and valuable road map to a successful business.

Every business has its own unique set of necessities, but when it comes to establishing a business plan, certain rules and patterns must be followed. There are key elements you should be aware of that investors, bankers, and other financial sources look for when considering a project for financing. This book explains these key elements, unlocks the door to successfully financing a business, and acts as a guideline for conducting research, compiling what you have learned, and assembling a comprehensive and thorough business plan.

Although most people associate writing a business plan with raising capital, there are other types of plans that focus specifically on the nature of the growing enterprise. These types of plans are called "strategic business plans" and are generally used and kept within the business. These plans are excellent tools for competing in today's tough business climate.

By writing your own business plan, you will be examining your business operations first-hand and, in the process, coming up with ways to improve them. Over a million new businesses are started every year in the United States. Unfortunately, only a small number of these businesses and potential business owners take the time to develop a sound business plan, and even fewer will actually follow the steps and strategies outlined in their plan.

This book shows you how to take what seems to be an arduous, time-consuming, unnecessary task and turn it into an exciting, rewarding, and profitable exercise. The information in this book is organized in the order of the sequence to be followed in writing your business plan. It includes details on how to research the market, where to find information, what kind of strategies to use, what potential financial resources are available, how the individuals capable of providing those resources will weigh the information you provide, and the importance they will place on certain items of information. You will learn how to be persuasive and effective when presenting your business plan, and how to be confident and informed as you navigate the competitive world of business. Chapter 1 is an overview that will give you all the important basics and get you in the right frame of mind to start working on your plan. After that, each chapter explains one individual component of a business plan and gives you plenty of writing space to develop your ideas as you read along. The last chapter is a sample plan for you to refer to as you read the book. Use it to gain a clearer understanding of what your own business plan should look like. For further guidance, see Appendix 2 and 3, where two additional business plans are given. Also, Appendix 1 lists a set of questions to help you compile your plan; if you answer them all, you'll have thought through most of the questions that are needed to write a comprehensive business plan. Feel free to make copies of Appendix 1 to take with you to classes or meetings, or during your preliminary research, to jot down these important answers all in one place.

When thinking about starting or developing a business, keep in mind how pervasive technology is in our daily lives, both professionally and personally. Computer software programs and the hardware required to run them are making our lives much easier. The Internet is an incredible tool for research, advertising, and providing timely information to customers as well as employees. Email is not only saving time and money, but it is also a marvelous tool for communicating. Instead of getting lost in voice mail, you can communicate in a manner that gets attention—often immediately. It is also a great way to maintain a record of what you say without it getting lost, misunderstood, or even forgotten.

Companies are also migrating to their own internal Internet, called an intranet. This is an internal Web that only allows employees with a current login or user identification, a password, and a secure network or dial-up connection to access company information. Some of the things that can be found on an intranet are corporate forms and updates, marketing materials, time sheets, expense reports, corporate telephone and email directories, annual reports, software that can be downloaded to local desktops, company calendar, company newsletter, and much, much more. The possibilities are endless!

The world of technology is ever changing. New tools, equipment, and techniques are available at almost any given time. It used to be that technology would replace itself every decade. Now a computer or the software used to run a computer can become obsolete in six to eighteen months. The businesses that stay ahead of the technology curve will be far more successful than those that do not. Even if a company can at least stay close to this ever-changing curve and take advantage of new technology when it is feasible, it will be leaps and bounds ahead of the competition. Don't get left behind while the world around you, including your competitors, takes full advantage of these tools and technologies.

As we mentioned, whenever you take a trip to an unknown or unfamiliar place, you should carry a map with you. Businesses also have unfamiliar and unknown terrain. Whether you are writing a business plan for the first time or the tenth time, this book will guide you through the important sequences and steps in a simple and highly effective manner, and get you the results that will allow you to compete in any business climate.

# Chapter 1

# Powerful Guidelines to Writing Your First Business Plan

*The will to win is worthless if you do not have the will to prepare.*
—Thane Yost

- ▶ **A few facts about business planning**
- ▶ **Consider a start-up's impact on your life**
- ▶ **The nuts and bolts of a business plan**
- ▶ **Focus on your Unique Selling Proposition (USP)**

When it comes to writing a business plan, most people think it's about as much fun as taking a trip to the dentist. They usually focus on the pain rather than the results. Let's face it, writing a good business plan takes a lot of time, patience, and thought, and many hours of research, writing, and editing. But think of the results! You will know your business (and yourself) better and be better assured that it will flourish. In addition, you will have a better chance of getting financing. Most importantly, you will know how to conduct business and compete at a more sophisticated level. The time invested in developing a business plan *can* make the difference.

Also consider the edge you will have over your competition. Countless businesses do not have a business plan. They are simply reacting to the conditions that exist, much like a sailboat haplessly setting out on a windless day—or, in other cases, a stormy day. The point is that when you take the time to fully develop a sound business plan, you will have a greater advantage in maneuvering and changing your course when the climate is not to your benefit.

## A Few Facts about Business Planning

About one million new businesses are started each year in America; of those, approximately two hundred thousand will survive five years. This translates into one in five businesses making it to their fifth anniversary. This is an alarming statistic! Why in the world would only one in five businesses in the "Land of Opportunity" survive for so short a period of time? There are several reasons, but the most common also happens to be the most controllable. There is no magic equation for success, but one basic rule holds true: A business owner who fails to plan also plans to fail.

**Think Outside the Box:** Advice about starting a business and developing a plan to help oversee it can come from any of a number of sources. Consider going to trade shows and other networking opportunities in your field and make it a goal to meet as many people as you can. You never know what might come of it.

A business plan helps entrepreneurs and business managers think through their strategies, balance their enthusiasm with facts, and recognize their limitations. It also helps avoid potentially disastrous errors like under-capitalizing, creating negative cash flow, hiring the wrong people, selecting the wrong location, and pursuing the wrong market. See Figure 1.1 below for a list of questions to ask yourself (and your partner, if you have one) when choosing your market.

A winning business plan requires time: fifty to one hundred hours to write an effective business plan, which would include research, documentation, analysis, and review. Keep this in mind, and remember that entrepreneurs should start planning at least six months before they initiate a new business. This takes into consideration the time you need to devote to start-up while working another job. Six months gives you time to sharpen and focus your business ideas, test your assumptions, and improve your management skills.

So dig in and begin your journey. This chapter gives you an overview of the essential elements that must be part of your task.

---

### Figure 1.1 YOUR NEW ENTERPRISE—BEFORE START-UP

**The type of business you pursue depends on a few important factors:**

- How much money do you have to invest?
- Can you attract other investors?
- What return do you expect?
- Where is your expertise?
- What do you like to do most?
- Are you willing to work hard and long hours?
- What are prominent consumer trends in your industry today?

## Consider a Start-Up's Impact on Your Life

Before venturing full-force into your start-up business, consider these possibilities. Your income may suffer, your work hours will multiply, and your family relationships may be strained. You will have expended your personal cash and possibly assumed a fair amount of debt. Most of the time, you may feel like you're running behind, and you may become more irritable or critical with people around you. You will see less of your friends and family; you may get more headaches, backaches, or stomachaches. You may feel guilty at times when you take time off from work. Your life, for a time, may truly be all work and no play.

Don't despair! These feelings and circumstances are a normal part of starting a business or embarking on a new project. Just don't give up. Developing a business plan is going to be very hard work, but if you do it right, wonderful things may result. So begin your research earnestly and objectively. Figure 1.2 on the next page alerts you to some good starting points.

## The Nuts and Bolts of a Business Plan

### Think about a Mission Statement

Once you have completed a good amount of research, you can begin to define your business, and writing a mission statement is an important step in further cementing your idea. A mission statement should be fifty words or less and outline what you will sell and to whom, and what will make your business different. (This is called your "Unique Selling Proposition," or USP, which we describe in detail at the end of this chapter.)

Here is an example of a mission statement:

> ### *Mission Statement*
> To provide useful, applicable solutions to business owners and managers in the areas of marketing, business planning, finance, accounting, and promotion, and to fully use our management team's experience and knowledge to increase the revenues of each of our clients' enterprises and companies.

## Figure 1.2: HOT INFORMATION SOURCES

**There are so many good sources of information to pull from when it comes to starting a business or strategizing about developing the one you already have. So start your research!**

- Your local chamber of commerce will assist you, whether you are a member or not.

- Trade shows are a one-stop shopping source for businesses, suppliers, and various consultants.

- Approach a trade association executive and ask him or her what is hot in the marketplace.

- Send a press release to as many trade magazine editors as possible.

- Also send those press releases to newspaper editors.

- Local networking meetings are tremendous sources for leads. Start your own if you have to.

- Federal, state, and university programs allow you to get up-to-date information while meeting new people at the same time.

- Check in with your state commissioner of economic development.

- S.C.O.R.E. (Service Corps of Retired Executives) will link you with an expert who has been there before.

- Check in with the U.S. Embassy in the country or countries you plan to do business with.

- Conduct research at businesses similar to yours in noncompetitive locations. You might want to use a magic phrase (such as "I've got a problem and I think you can help me") to start a conversation.

- The Foreign Trade Zones Board is an entity that reviews and approves applications to import foreign goods.

- Small Business Administration (SBA) is a government-run association created to help small businesses such as yours succeed.

- The Internet: What was once a tool for the government to send and receive data is now a powerful and fast commercial tool to obtain information on almost any subject you can possibly think of.

Also place your mission statement on page 89 in Chapter 11, which describes the executive summary.

---

**QUICK Tip**

Write a Compelling Mission Statement: A mission statement is a company's formal, written declaration of its reason for existing. A good mission statement captures an organization's purpose, customer orientation, business philosophy, and values in language that is as clear and broad as possible. A mission statement is usually one or two sentences long.

---

## Name Your Business

A compelling component of your business idea is the name you put to it. You may already have an idea for your business's name, but also be sure to think and rethink that name once you have conducted market research.

Our advice is to keep the name straightforward and descriptive, and make it as distinctive as possible. Avoid grandiose, overworked adjectives. Your business name should be like a headline to an article. It should describe who you are and what you do. A dangerous marketing mistake is to make your prospects and potential customers guess what it is that you do. For example, Bob's Hardware Store says so much more than Bob's Enterprises. Ambassador Pizza works much more effectively than Ambassador Foods. You end up spending much more time and precious capital marketing your product or service when the customer has to guess what you do. Most businesses do not have that luxury, so have some type of descriptive word in your company name that will benefit you. Let the companies with deep pockets promote ambiguous names to create their own identity.

## Consider All Uses of a Business Plan

Your business plan is the heart and soul of your operation and the most important document you provide to any lending institution or potential investor. It explains all the financing you need and, most importantly, it will give your financial sources persuasive information about your venture.

Please keep that in mind and convince yourself that proper business planning is an absolute necessity.

Business Plans Test Validity: People often develop preliminary business plans for a number of different businesses before actually deciding on and starting a business of their own. This is a smart way of spending time with your idea to objectively determine if it will fly. Remember, there is no money lost on an abandoned business plan.

Also remember that your business plan is a multipurpose document. A comprehensive and realistic business plan will help you accomplish many essential objectives. It will help you:

1. *Take charge of your entrepreneurial life.* A business plan is evidence of your initiative. It shows that you have discipline to focus your energy on an important project. It also shows that you understand how to achieve progress and growth, solve problems along the way, and realize your ultimate goals. The business plan is the foundation that provides pillars for your vision and allows you to structure your ideas into reality.

2. *Lay out a master blueprint.* A business plan is to an entrepreneur what a set of detailed architectural drawings is to a builder. It shows you the logical progression of steps needed to reach your established goal. It may also help you consider an alternate and possibly better route. A business plan is a powerful management tool.

3. *Communicate your master plan to members of your team.* A business plan allows you to communicate to your colleagues a step-by-step agenda for reaching your goals. Some portions of a business plan can also be used in training and coordinating meetings, as well as teaching staff what their role and accountability will be in making your business function successfully.

4. *Attract money to your project.* Potential suppliers of capital and other needed resources (such as bankers, brokers, investors, future partners, and the like) will place great value on your business plan as they determine whether or not to participate in your venture (see Figure 1.3).

Your ability to create trust and respect can be greatly enhanced through interpersonal contact with these potential suppliers of capital. However, you may not even get a chance to get to know these people on a personal basis; therefore, you must have a professional document to present in written form. Your business plan will be your initial selling tool—your business résumé—when attracting lenders to participate with you in your venture.

---

**Figure 1.3:**
### KNOW WHAT POTENTIAL SUPPLIERS OF CAPITAL LOOK AT FIRST

**There are four critical areas of a business plan investors consider heavily before they involve themselves in your venture. Make sure you build a strong case for each of these critical areas:**

1. Your management team
2. Your current and projected financial statements
3. Your products and services
4. Your marketing plan

---

## Management Team

Your management team is very important. Potential investment sources place a tremendous amount of importance on the team of managers who will be making crucial day-to-day decisions. The success or failure of your enterprise depends on the experience, maturity, and common sense of you, your partners, your board of directors, and your management staff.

Any management team needs balance. This balance gives you the ability to provide the organization with four essential elements:

1. Planning
2. Organization
3. Control
4. Leadership

Balance within a management team, as a whole, includes the behavioral, technical, and conceptual skills applicable to the development, production, and delivery of both current and future products and services. At a minimum, the management team must have or develop skills in management, marketing, finance, and operations.

The strength of your management team must be diligently articulated in your business plan. A company with a formal structure will greatly enhance its ability to raise capital and achieve its goals in less time, and with far less expense.

Use honesty in your judgment of yourself and each member of the management team. Don't allow yourself to sway from truth or reality. If your management team is weak in any of the above areas, consider bringing in top-notch, experienced professionals to help you and bring in overall inspiration. Outside professionals can offer your enterprise tremendous leverage—without carrying them on your payroll. Advisors you may need throughout your planning efforts are a competent attorney, management consultant, accountant, insurance agent, and banker. A marketing consultant could also be helpful—he or she may save you time, money, and misspent effort. These experts will help you, your management team, and your business develop and grow.

## Your Current and Projected Financial Statements

When it comes to thinking about your business's finances, you need to consider your current and projected future situation. Determine your cash needs, project your expenses, and review your sales and profit objectives.

You should also prepare a preliminary balance sheet. List your assets and liabilities to create a snapshot of what your company looks like at a given moment. Your balance sheet is a necessary tool for your banker and your accountant.

The financial projections that you document in your business plan should be well thought out. Plan on devoting a fair amount of time to developing these. If you have to tell the investor to ask your accountant about something regarding your financial position, you project a less-than-solid business to the investor. To avoid this, include financial projections on:

1. Your profit-and-loss statement
2. Your balance sheet
3. Your cash-flow statement

When calculating your projections for the future, at a minimum, illustrate monthly figures for the first two years and annual projections for years three through five.

### Hooking up with the Right People:
Scout out a university-run business plan competition or class to help you fine-tune your pitch for capital. The professionals involved in a program such as this usually consist of a few venture capitalists who will be able to give you excellent guidance on the financial details of your plan.

## Your Products and Services
Your products or services are obviously very important when attracting potential sources of capital. In your business plan, be sure to discuss the unique and specific characteristics of your products and services:

• How do they differ from similar products and services?
• What customer reactions may be anticipated due to these characteristics?
• How will you satisfy customer needs and wants?

Describe any unique value-added characteristics your products and services provide to the customer and how these will give your company a competitive edge. If your product or service has evolved over the past few years, explain how and why.

Describe how the product works or how the service is used. Will your product save your customers time or money? Will your product or service generate more profits for your customers? If so, how?

Have any tests or case studies been performed that will help you back up your claims? Obtain that vital information and document it in your plan.

What is the product or service's life cycle? Explain it to the investor. You may even want to create a simple chart covering the life cycles of your products and services. Also include the time factors influencing your ability to make money and the effects of economic cycles.

Typical stages are:

1. *Introduction stage*: An intense marketing campaign introduces a new or unique product or service.

2. *Growth stage*: Sales begin and growth occurs.

3. *Maturity stage*: The market begins to be saturated with the unique product or service. Competition increases as awareness of product becomes common.

4. *Decline stage*: Newer, more unique, and more advanced products enter the market. Loyal customers continue to buy your product or service. Not-so-loyals begin to look at alternatives, and eventually may shift their business to the newer items.

Discuss your plans for the next generation of products and services that will be introduced in the near future.

Be prepared to contact several different investment sources and groups to discover which capital sources will be most interested in your particular venture. For example, some suppliers of finances only look at real estate transactions. Others may only consider franchise concepts, while others may wish to invest in a manufacturing enterprise.

**QUICK Tip**

Attend to Packaging: The business plan should be clean, conservative, simple, well-prepared, clearly written, error free, and appropriately bound. Your plan should look impressive, but not overly slick. Let the visual form reflect the quality of the content. If you are presenting the business plan to prospective financial sources, you should bind the material in such a way that it will open flat on a desk. For in-office use, the business plan should be organized in a three-ring binder, where updates can be easily incorporated.

## Your Marketing Plan

Your marketing plan is next on the list of importance. This area requires a fair amount of study and analysis on your part. Although it may seem a lengthy task at the onset, you can still have a lot of fun with it. This is when you find out who is out there, what the competition offers and what they don't offer, whether or not your product or service will outsell the competition, and what Unique Selling Proposition (USP) you have over your competitors.

You may even discover that the timing is not right for your enterprise and it would be beneficial not to go ahead with your plans. This would not be a negative bit of information to find. The time and money you would save by waiting for a better time or pursuing another market would be invaluable. Your future enterprise may depend on what the market dictates after a carefully designed marketing analysis. So have fun with this section and enjoy seeing what is out there!

A market analysis describes the existing marketplace in which you plan to operate your business. When doing a marketing analysis, you are hoping to define what specific segment of the market will purchase your product or service. Key points for defining the market segment for your products and services are:

1. Product features
2. Lifestyle of your targeted customers

3. Geographical location
4. Cyclical factors

How many competitors share your market? How is the share of the market distributed among the major participants? Is the market growing at a rapid rate? What are the major trends toward the development of the shared marketplace? Summarize your view of the trends and the implied opportunities from your market analysis.

In this section, you will want to list the strengths and weaknesses of your product and service. When covering your strengths, you need to be sure to place at least as much emphasis on marketing your product as on your product itself, if not more. List several distinct advantages over the competition in the following areas:

1. Actual performance
2. Quality and reliability
3. Production efficiencies
4. Distribution
5. Pricing
6. Promotion
7. Public image or reputation
8. Business relationships or references

If you know of any weaknesses in your product or service, list those also and show what steps you are taking to alleviate the problem(s).

Developing a marketing strategy is the art and science of planning for and implementing a promotional campaign that will generate sales for your enterprise. Such strategies are designed to enhance, promote, and support the advantages, features, and benefits of your products and services.

Your marketing section should be designed with one word in mind: strategy. When thinking about a strategy, you must take into consideration your business activities, strengths, and direction. What type of strategy would you put together if your very existence depended on it? A good strategy could save you. See Figure 1.4 on the next page for a list of questions to ask while developing your marketing plan.

Figure 1.4: **MARKETING QUESTIONS TO BRAINSTORM BY**

**There are several questions you should pay attention to when developing a marketing plan.**

- What can be said about your competitors' products or services that will change your customer's minds?
- What is your Unique Selling Proposition?
- What strategies will you use to promote your products and services?
- Will you use television and radio?
- Would it benefit you to conduct seminars or participate in trade shows?
- Will you use telemarketing and/or outside sales representatives?
- Do you need to hire a public relations agency?
- Have you considered direct mail?
- Will you use brochures and flyers?
- Will you sell your products and services locally, nationally, or internationally?
- What other creative ideas will you come up with to generate leads?
- Are your strategies consistent with your evaluation of the marketplace and your capabilities?
- Have you defined your targeted market into a narrow window, or does your product appeal to a large market?
- Are your strategies based on facts or assumptions?
- Is your appraisal of the competition open-minded and honest?
- Is the expected return on investment sufficient to justify the risks?
- Have you thoroughly examined strategies your competitors are using? Could some of their strategies be adapted to your environment?
- Is your strategy legal?

Your strategy should be defined in such terms as to capture your share of the market in as little time as possible. With this in mind, how will your customers perceive your company and products relative to the competition? This is critical and worth repeating. How will your customers perceive your company and products relative to the competition? A good way to find out is to ask them. Conduct a market survey. This is an easy and inexpensive way to find out the answer to this important question.

## QUICK Tip

Present the Business Plan Skillfully and Graphically: Consider using projection technology and similar support equipment when presenting your business plan to prospective funders. Presenting economic and chart-oriented information in attractive visual ways helps solidify your position. Also, it speeds up presentations, makes the important facts quickly accessible, and reflects well on your ability as an effective business manager.

## Focus on Your Unique Selling Proposition (USP)

It is important to understand how vital it is to adopt your own USP and implement it from everyone to the president through the sales team to your clerical staff. Everybody within an organization should have a solid understanding of what sets you apart from the competition.

Your USP is that single, unique advantage, benefit, essence, appeal, or big promise that holds your product or service out to the prospective customer—one that no other competitor offers or advertises. You should be able to articulate, in one or two crisp, clear paragraphs, the Unique Selling Proposition of your business's product or service. The backbone of your entire business concept, your USP needs serious consideration. You would do well do ponder the following comments:

• Your USP is literally the unique advantage that distinguishes your business from everyone else's. This is a concept that your entire enterprise should be built around.

- Without a USP, you cannot build a consistent and effective marketing campaign.
- Identify the unique advantage(s) you should build your marketing efforts around. You need to define it in a clear paragraph. Once you have developed your own Unique Selling Proposition, formulating a winning marketing strategy will come much easier. Therefore, tell it accurately, intelligently, and in the most straightforward way possible
- A USP may be that your product is made entirely of all-natural ingredients or has a warranty for double the amount of time of your competitors' warranties. Maybe you offer three times more follow-up efforts in calling, writing to, or actually visiting your customers after they purchase your product or service. Possibly your product is completely handmade, the only product in your area, or the competition will take years to produce something as good as what you offer. Maybe your business stays open two hours longer than all of your competitors' businesses for added convenience to your customers.

You probably get the idea. Go ahead! Create a USP that lets people feel like they cannot live a moment longer without your product or service. You may be surprised how easy this is.

# Chapter 2

# The First Pages

*What you can do, or dream you can do, begin
it. Begin it and the work will be completed.*
—Göethe

- ▶ **Cover sheet**
- ▶ **Table of contents**
- ▶ **Executive summary**

It is important to note that the format of your business plan, the amount of detail it contains, and the visual presentation may vary according to the intended use and readership. Chapters 2 through 12 are intended to show you the elements needed to compile a winning plan that will attract potential financial resources, as well as provide valuable information regarding the establishment and growth of your venture. In this chapter, we cover the items you should consider including in the first few pages of your plan.

# Cover Sheet

If you are appealing to prospective investors, money brokers, bankers, and venture capitalists, include a cover sheet, preferably on company stationery, displaying company emblems and logos. This will help place your content in a framework of legitimacy.

Keep your cover sheet as simple as possible. Identify yourself, your business, and the institution or party to which you are addressing your appeal, and include the date the plan is submitted. Here is a checklist of items that may be included:

1.  Business's basic information, including:
    a.  Name of business
    b.  Location, address
    c.  Telephone number
    d.  Contact person(s), including titles
    e.  Website address and email address
2.  Business paragraph. A quick and essential promotional description of the business's goals, potential, and outlook.
3.  Capital required. The current and anticipated future financial needs of the business.
4.  Name(s) of the person(s) recommending you to the investor.
5.  Include a paragraph notifying the investor that all information provided is proprietary, strictly confidential, and may not be released without your written authorization.

See the next page for an example of a business plan cover sheet.

PRESENTED TO:
THE VENTURA CAPITAL FUNDING GROUP

A BUSINESS PLAN FOR:

Home Improvements, Inc.
1234 East Main Street
Suite 1012
Anywhere, Arizona 85999
www.homeimprovementsinc.com
info@homeimprovementsinc.com

January 2005

Contact:
Michael J. Swann
President

This business plan is copy number _____

Get the Order Right: Experts always tell you to write the introduction, executive summary, and conclusion of your business plan after you've completed all other sections. Saving these sections until you are done will give you the perspective you need to write them well.

## Table of Contents

A table of contents will help your prospective lender understand the material you are presenting and also make a statement about you. It will show that you are organized, thorough, sensitive to the needs of those you are approaching, and able to manage the big picture. Type up the table of contents when you are completely done with your plan. A sample table of contents follows on page 22.

### QUICK Tip

Be Realistic: Build your business plan with a sense of realism and practicality. Do your homework carefully and think through every detail that could have a bearing on the success of your project. Your business plan should be a carefully crafted, practical document geared toward performance, and not a speculative piece of fortune-telling.

## Executive Summary

This portion of the business plan must be designed to capture and hold the interest of the party to whom the plan is being presented. It is here that you capture your public's interest—it can make you or break you. Make sure it can be read in a few minutes. Make it sell! Keep it to within two to five typed pages.

This critical executive summary encapsulates the entire business plan in a few paragraphs by giving the most succinct statement possible of the nature and objectives of your business, such as:

- Its mission
- Its Unique Selling Proposition
- Your projections for the future (sales, costs, and profits)
- Your needs (inventory, land, building, equipment, working capital, and other resources)
- Procedures and timetable for repaying investors
- The capital you are requesting

This summary is a crystallization of the entire business plan in an overview format. Don't neglect this section. It will demonstrate that you can clearly focus on your goals and state, in no-nonsense fashion, who you are, what you want, and where you are going.

Since the executive summary serves to summarize your whole plan, it is often the last section written, after all of the other pieces have been put together. A sample executive summary is on pages 100–105. An example of a mission statement that could appear in the executive summary is as follows:

---

### Mission Statement

To provide customers with high-quality exterior aluminum siding and double-pane windows where we can be proud of the integrity and craftsmanship of each product sold to the end-user, and offer superior customer service throughout the warranty phases of the product, remembering that each customer may be a tremendous source of referral business to our company.

---

## Table of Contents

# Chapter **3**

# General Company Description

*The person who minds nobody's business but his own is probably a millionaire.*
—Anonymous

- ▶ **Context of your business**
- ▶ **Profile of your business**
- ▶ **Profile of your specific market**
- ▶ **Anticipated challenges and planned responses**

# Context of Your Business

This portion of your business plan will provide a big picture perspective of the industry to which your business belongs and prepare the reader to better understand how your business fits into this picture. It should include:

- *Industry background.* Describe how big the category is, the different segments of it, and the industry trends.
- *Growth potential.* In light of the trends you just described, provide a statement (in dollars) of the future growth potential of the industry in which you are competing.
- *New products and developments.* What new developments have arisen in the recent past that will make your product or service more attractive to the consumer?
- *Economic trends.* Describe evidence that spending trends are favorable to the industry.
- *Industry outlook and forecasts.* Describe the future of the industry according to industry leaders, experts, economists, government forecasters, and other authoritative sources.

---

### *Business Background*

In a published report by the Improved Contracting Unit of Westeck International, the exterior aluminum siding market is growing at a rapid rate. The report claims that "the market for siding in the United States is virtually untapped. The United States is a very immature market with tremendous growth potential."

Over the past three years, companies have developed and shown that additional features can be provided within this type of industry. These companies have focused on the use of technological advances to steadily improve the quality of aluminum in exterior siding.

These advances and the positive reports made by New Consumer Product Reports, which states that firms selling home-value-added products will prosper greatly in the coming decade, are encouraging testimony of our future in this area.

# Profile of Your Business

It is important to remember that throughout your business plan, you must inform the reader of all major factors, positive and negative, that may have an effect on the outcome of your organization. This section should provide the reader with the concept of how your business works and why it has a unique chance to shine in the marketplace. Make sure to ask yourself the following questions:

- What is the precise nature of your business?
- How have you developed your products and services?
  Give a brief history.
- What are the economic trends? Give evidence that spending trends are favorable to the industry.
- What is the organizational detail of your business?
- What are the factors that influence your business? Be sure to include local economic factors, seasonality, and dependence on special vendors or suppliers.
- What are your plans for research and development? Include:
  1. The nature of your test-marketing procedures
  2. Results achieved
  3. Product development
  4. Legal control of process and/or product
- Do you have contracts and agreements such as resale agreements, service contracts, or leases? Identify them here and include copies in the appendix.
- What are your operational procedures?
  1. For ventures involving manufacturing a product, consider:
     a. Physical space requirements
     b. Machinery and equipment
     c. Raw materials
     d. Inventory and supplies
     e. Personnel requirements
     f. Capital estimates
  2. For ventures involving wholesaling and/or retailing, consider:
     a. Physical space requirements

      b. Purchasing procedures and plans

      c. Inventory system

      d. Staff and equipment

      e. Training

      f. Credentials

**QUICK Tip**

Invest in Help: Never underestimate the importance of hiring professional help as you develop your approach to your business. The services you hire may include those of an attorney, management consultant, accountant, insurance agent, marketing consultant, and banker. If you do not have enough money to get outside help, then you probably do not have enough money to launch a successful business.

## Profile of Your Specific Market

Accurately defining your target market requires a lot of time and effort. In structuring your market profile, make sure you have done your homework and research with great care and due diligence. Don't assume that your target exists or that it can be created in a relatively short period of time.

> ### *Current Business Position*
>
> Currently, the Arizona market distribution is shared by nine participants. Home Improvement Inc. enjoys a 30 percent share of this market. There are four other major competitors that share approximately 60 percent, and the remaining competitors share a combined total of 10 percent of the market.
>
>     The stability of this market segment is expected to increase; however, some volatility has been introduced to the market with the current national recession.

## Define Your Specific Market

- State precisely who the consumers of your products or services are.
- Note their geographical scope, including size and population.
- Consider the growth potential of your target market.
- Evaluate your ability to satisfy the market's demands.
- Know how your business plan will enable you to attract new customers while keeping the customers you have.

When developing a profile of your target market, it is important to remember that your research will determine the strength of your analysis. The time you spend on this section should be spent wisely. Your local library and your telephone will be your strongest allies, so use them to their fullest. Also take advantage of the information and statistics already available in books, directories, and case studies. Thorough research will impress potential investors more than you can believe.

---

### *Demographics of Target Market*

#### STAY-AT-HOME PARENT

| | |
|---|---|
| Age | 35–65 |
| Income | Fixed |
| Sex | Female or Male |
| Family | Full nest |
| Geographic | Suburban |
| Occupation | Stay-at-home parent |
| Attitude | Security-minded |

---

# Anticipated Challenges and Planned Responses

This section of the plan sets forth your contingency strategies for dealing with anticipated barriers and challenges. These are some of the main types:

1. **The competition factor**. Establish the following for each of your key competitors:
   a. The similarities and differences when compared with your business
   b. Their strengths and weaknesses
   c. Your "competitive edge" (your Unique Selling Proposition), enabling you to prevail and stay on course
   d. Your insight into how the competition will try to block your market entry and how you will respond

---

### Competitive Overview

Competitive threats today come from three primary competitors and three other dealers in Arizona. HII's products perform in virtually all situations in which there is a home or office where siding and windows can be added. The ability to offer increased "curb appeal" in addition to providing insulation is a unique attraction to a customer.

Our research indicates that the performance of these products is superior to anything else on the market today. In all comparisons, the HII products provide more features and have superior performance than competitive products. A complete technical comparison is available.

---

2. **The vulnerability factor**. Consider:
   a. Product obsolescence
   b. Cheaper products on the horizon
   c. Cyclical trends in the marketplace
   d. Possible economic downturn in the future
   e. Turnover of key employees
   f. Seasonality of your products and services
   g. Compensation benefits package to employees

## *Potential Vulnerabilities*

There are handicaps inherent in the market. The notable marketplace disadvantage is the price the customer is willing to pay for home beauty and energy efficiency. The average job will cost $13,000 if the entire home is covered with siding and double-pane windows. This cost must be justified in the mind of the consumer.

Corporate weaknesses, due in part to present economic factors, include limited sales personnel. However, steps are being taken to alleviate this as healthier economic trends emerge, justifying expansion in this area.

3. **The legal factors**. Consider:
    a. License requirements that you must satisfy or maintain
    b. Restrictions and regulations under which you must operate, given the nature of your business
    c. Future changes in legal or governmental policies that may affect your business and how you intend to respond
    d. Any governmental agencies with whom you must register

## *Legal Issues*

Completed tests have shown that HII aluminum siding has been subjected to tests of impact against both hard and soft objects in accordance with common rules for Product Durability Testing Requirements set forth by U.S. regulations. The test resulted in performance far superior to the minimum required regulations.

4. **The protection issues**. Include:
    a. Patents, copyrights, trademarks, and other protection procedures
    b. Steps to assure business secrets are preserved

If you are a start-up business—or an established business that has new products, ideas, or technology that will improve someone's standard of living—and you want to place your products on the market, your products should be patented or trademarked, and all your written material should be copyrighted.

The two basic kinds of patents are *mechanical* and *design*. The distinction between the two is that a mechanical patent is used when the concept involves a new product that operates mechanically and is something no one has ever developed before. A design patent is an improvement to a previously patented product, such that its design makes the existing product better. However, there is the possibility of infringing on the older patent if all you did was change the design while maintaining the original mechanics.

The automobile industry gives ample examples of both types of patents. Design changes are radical and continuous as the marketplace dictates. Each change in design is patented and lasts for three years, while mechanical patents last for seventeen years and can be renewed thereafter.

For your protection, we strongly suggest seeking the council of an attorney who specializes in patents, trademarks, copyrights, and secret formulas.

---

### Key Man Contingency

The founders and key managers of HII have combined experiences exceeding twenty-five years in the siding and distribution areas. The strength of the management team stems from the combined expertise in both management and sales areas, producing outstanding results over the past year.

The leadership and alignment characteristics of the HII's management team have resulted in broad and flexible goal-setting to meet the ever-changing demands of the quickly moving marketplace that requires our products. This is evident when the team responds to situations requiring new and innovative capabilities.

5. **The key man contingency**. Involves:
   a. The depth of your management team
   b. Management procedures in place to assure continuity of leadership
   c. Plans for responding to the loss of important personnel
6. **Staffing**. Include:
   a. Personnel needs you anticipate over time, including head-count requirements, training, benefits, and expansion, and how these needs will be met
   b. Policies on minority issues
   c. Policies on temporary versus permanent staff
   d. Policies on harassment, racism, or prejudices of any kind

It is important to remember that the information covered in this section must demonstrate that you have covered the problem bases and have carefully crafted contingency plans in place. The information will provide your business plan with more credibility than you think. Be practical and reasonable. Show that you have really done your homework.

---

### Staffing Overview

The HII development team recognizes that additional staff is required to properly support marketing, sales, research and development, and other support functions.

Currently, HII is composed of eight people. Over the next five years, fifty people will be required to meet the demands of the projected market. These staff requirements will include personnel in the following areas:

- management
- marketing
- sales
- engineering
- customer relations
- administration
- manufacturing
- skilled assembly labor

# Chapter 4

# Present Situation

*This time, like all other times, is a very good one if we but know what to do with it.*
—Ralph Waldo Emerson

- Give a snapshot of your situation
- Calculate your Current Ratio
- Calculate your Quick Ratio

Whether you are engaged in a start-up or you are already in business, in this section, you will clearly define how you have come to your current position. Start by identifying how your idea was conceived up to today. If you are already operating, give a summary of your personnel, business activities, operation methods, and any other nonmonetary factors you think are important. You'll also have to buckle down and be brutally honest about your present financial circumstances. Describe your financial circumstances. What do you have by way of personal and business assets and liabilities?

A Multipurpose Document: Depending on your needs and your goals, your business plan will be read by a series of people. To attract funding, you will be selling your idea to outside investors, venture capitalists, and the bank. You might also use your plan to attract talented future employees. And beyond that, you are writing your business plan to sell yourself on your business idea. Promise yourself that you will deal honestly and objectively with each issue that arises during your research, including the possibility of abandoning the idea altogether.

## Give a Snapshot of Your Situation

Answer the following questions to develop this section:

Explain the current market environment. Is it undergoing changes in technology, demographics, competition, customers, or financial conditions?

_____

_____

_____

_____

_____

What is the present stage of your industry: infancy, intermediate, or mature?

_____

_____

_____

_____

_____

Are there factors that could contribute to the growth or decline of your product? Indicate both the weak and strong points here. It will show that you have done your homework.

_____

_____

_____

_____

_____

_____

Where are your products assembled or manufactured?

_____

_____

_____

_____

_____

What is your product's average life cycle?

_____

_____

_____

_____

_____

_____

With regards to pricing and profitability, are current prices from suppliers increasing, decreasing, or remaining constant?

_____

_____

_____

_____

_____

_____

Indicate how you plan to make whatever adjustments are necessary to manage these possible changes in prices.

_____

_____

_____

_____

_____

How are your current or potential customers using your products/services? If your business is a start-up enterprise, how will it use your products/services?

_____

_____

_____

_____

_____

Where will your main distribution center be? Do you have any plans to open other offices and distribution centers? If so, indicate when and where.

_____

_____

_____

_____

_____

**Learn with Others:** Be on the lookout for free and low-cost workshops and classes to teach you the basics of creating a business plan, often given by banks, the SBDC (Small Business Development Centers), universities, and business planning firms. This would also be a great networking opportunity. So smile, put your best face forward, and see what comes up.

Give some additional information about your management team. Are they all in place? Will you need to hire additional managers or consult with outside consultants?

_____

_____

_____

_____

_____

Finally, provide some information about your current financial resources.

• Current cash available is

$ _____ as of _____

# Calculate Your Current Ratio

• *Current Ratio* is current assets divided by current liabilities. The larger the number, the better the margin of safety for covering current liabilities. A ratio of 2.0 or better is considered good:

$$\frac{\text{Current Assets}}{\text{Current Liabilities}} \quad = \quad \underline{\hspace{4cm}}$$

# Calculate Your Quick Ratio

• *Quick Ratio* is cash plus accounts receivable divided by current liabilities. The larger the number, the better the protection for short-term creditors. A ratio of 1.0 or better is taken as a statement that the business is in a liquid condition:

$$\frac{\text{Cash and Equivalents} + \text{Accounts Receivable} + \text{Notes Receivable}}{\text{Total Current Liabilities}}$$

$$= \quad \underline{\hspace{4cm}}$$

# Chapter 5

# Objectives Section

*Our aspirations are our possibilities.*
—Robert Browning

- ▶ **Understand what you want and need to accomplish**
- ▶ **Record your objectives**

In this section, you will develop short- and long-term goals for your business. This is when you need to formulate a vision of where you want to be in a few years. Be specific and use percentages, figures, and timelines. Make sure that you balance enthusiasm with realism. It is a good idea to use checks and balances when you visualize your company's progress. In order to achieve your goals, set a few simple objectives for each year, first through fifth.

With these ideas in mind, begin writing down what it is you want to achieve.

## Understand What You Want and Need to Accomplish

Are your long-term objectives to stay a one-person shop or to build a large company with several hundred employees?

_____

_____

_____

_____

_____

Do you want your company to go public and sell its stock?

_____

_____

_____

_____

_____

### QUICK Tip

Getting Good Advice: When thinking about getting advice to run your business, consider turning to retired professionals in your field. They've been there before and can probably give you a good perspective. If you cannot find someone in your area, try hooking up with an individual through www.score.org.

Do you want to pass the leadership down to your children, grandchildren, or great-grandchildren?

_____

_____

_____

_____

_____

_____

What would you accomplish with additional capital: open new offices, purchase equipment, hire key personnel, or expand your marketing and advertising?

_____

_____

_____

_____

_____

_____

Will you develop a stronger network of suppliers and/or buyers as time goes on? How?

_____

_____

_____

_____

_____

_____

Will you become a manufacturer at any time? When?

_____

_____

_____

_____

_____

Write down what your intermediate goals are.

_____

_____

_____

_____

_____

_____

What profits do you expect to generate in years one through five?

_____

_____

_____

_____

_____

_____

In order for you to achieve your immediate goals, do you have any debts that must be restructured or paid down? Explain why in detail here.

_____

_____

_____

_____

_____

What will be your expected net profits after tax from sales each year? Take these net after-tax profits for a period of five years and show the total for that period of time.

_____

_____

_____

_____

_____

_____

Next, indicate total sales revenue for the same period of time.

_____

_____

_____

_____

**Alert!**

It's Not All Smooth Sailing: A business plan should be optimistic, of course, but never shy away from addressing the risks involved in your business idea. Be up-front and honest, and do not avoid the problem areas. Investors want to know that you've thought through the potential roadblocks and have a firm plan in place for how to overcome them.

# Record Your Objectives

Finally, write down at least ten objectives or goals you envision for your business.

1. _____

_____

_____

2. _____

_____

_____

3. _____

_____

_____

4. _____

_____

_____

5. _____

_____

_____

6. _____

_____

_____

7. _____

_____

_____

8. _____

_____

_____

9. _____

_____

_____

10. _____

_____

_____

# Chapter 6

# Product/Service Section

*Hide not your talents. They for use were made.*
*What's a sundial in the shade?*
—Benjamin Franklin

- Description of your product or service
- Added value
- Tests and approvals
- Product or service life cycle
- Trademarks and copyrights

In this section, you must clearly identify your products and/or services and explain all aspects of the purchasing, manufacturing, packaging, and distribution of these products and/or services. It will be important to make sure that they can be easily recognizable and understood by lending organizations.

Potential lenders and investment groups will lend capital only if they have confidence that the business concept has been clearly researched, identified, calculated, and thoroughly thought out.

## Description of Your Product or Service

In concise language, explain all important information regarding your products and/or service.

_____

_____

_____

_____

_____

_____

_____

_____

_____

_____

_____

_____

_____

_____

_____

_____

_____

_____

_____

_____

_____

_____

 **Create a Unique Selling Proposition (USP):** If you have a competitive edge, you have an advantage over your competitor, so emphasize it boldly. Make it your selling point and direct consumers to associate their needs with your USP at the expense of your competitors.

## Added Value

List and explain all the value-added features your product/service has. It is important to state clearly why your product/service is such a great item: What makes it unique? What sets it apart from the competition? Why would a customer buy from you?

_____

_____

_____

_____

_____

_____

_____

_____

_____

_____

_____

_____

_____

_____

_____

_____

_____

_____

_____

_____

_____

_____

## Tests and Approvals

List and explain all test ratings, approvals by government regulations, and the like that add substance to your product/service.

_____
_____
_____
_____
_____
_____
_____
_____
_____
_____
_____
_____
_____
_____
_____
_____
_____

## Product or Service Life Cycle

Identify product life, warranty, guarantee, etc., that cover each product/ service provided.

_____
_____
_____
_____
_____
_____
_____
_____
_____
_____

# Trademarks and Copyrights

List and describe all trademarks, patents, copyrights, and licenses owned or used. Help the lender assess the value of these additional assets.

_____
_____
_____
_____
_____
_____
_____
_____
_____
_____
_____
_____
_____
_____
_____
_____
_____
_____
_____
_____
_____
_____
_____

## QUICK Tip

Everyday Technology: Remember, the Internet, email, and intranets are rapidly becoming as common as a telephone number and a fax machine. Don't get left behind while the world around you, including your competitors, takes full advantage of these tools and technologies.

# Chapter 7

# Market Analysis

*Concentration is my motto. First honesty,*
*then industry, then concentration.*
—Andrew Carnegie

- ▸ **Do your homework**
- ▸ **Market strengths and weaknesses**
- ▸ **Customer profile**
- ▸ **Competition**

In this section, you should clearly identify your market. It is very important to show all relevant data that verifies you have carefully researched the market. Potential lenders and investment groups must be clearly convinced that the market you have identified is feasible for the distribution of your product or service.

---

### QUICK Tip

Expand Your Research: Market research doesn't involve only a library and the Internet. Hit the streets and the Yellow Pages and research businesses that are similar to yours. If you are in the service sector, pretend you are a customer and meet with as many service providers as you can. If you are opening a cafe, hit all the cafes in your area. Be cheerful and curious and say that you love their bakery and want to know who their supplier is. If you are opening a storefront, pay close attention to a similar store and monitor who shops there and whether or not customers walk out with a package in hand.

## Do Your Homework

Doing research will help identify your market, including competitors, market share, potential market share, market stability, market share and growth, and the success of the products and services in other markets. Include supporting documentation from third-party independent sources, such as magazine and newspaper articles, books, trade reports, government statistics, and surveys.

As a first step, describe the market. Provide a history, as well as information about the dollar volume involved, any recent trends in the market, and an analysis of your current position in the market.

_____

_____

_____

_____

_____

_____
_____
_____
_____
_____
_____
_____
_____
_____
_____

**QUICK Tip**

Extensive Research Will Serve You Well: Remember that writing a business plan actually involves far more research than it does writing. You absolutely must understand where your business fits in the marketplace before sitting down with that paper and pen.

## Market Strengths and Weaknesses

Identify marketing strengths, such as sources of advertising and promotion, public awareness, and public acceptance.

_____
_____
_____
_____
_____
_____
_____
_____
_____

Identify market weaknesses, such as possible lack of public acceptance and per-capita income.

_____

_____

_____

_____

_____

_____

_____

**Alert!**

Who Is Your Target Audience? The demographic you define as your customer base will never be "everyone," nor is it "all men" or "all women." Make sure you understand your customer and present a clear picture of who specifically will purchase your product and why.

## Customer Profile

Identify your customers (including the decision-maker), their per capita income, age, sex, family, geographic location, occupation, attitude, and so on.

What is your customer profile? (Give details on your typical customers.)

**If your customer is a business:**

Type of business_____

_____

Size of business (annual revenue) _____

_____

Geographical area(s) (number of locations) _____

_____

Number of employees _____

_____

Business structure (corporation, sole proprietorship, etc.) _____

_____

Years in business  _____

_____

**If your customer is an individual:**

Age _____

_____

Income  _____

_____

Sex _____

_____

Occupation_____

_____

Family size _____

_____

Culture  _____

_____

Education  _____

_____

# Competition

Identify all competitors. Describe your company plan to effectively compete and gain market share. Include strengths and weaknesses of your competitors and demonstrate their specific strategies. Provide charts, graphs, and data to support your claims.

Who is your competition?

1. _____
2. _____
3. _____
4. _____
5. _____
6. _____
7. _____
8. _____

How is your competition promoting its product or service?

_____
_____
_____
_____
_____
_____
_____
_____
_____
_____
_____

What are your competitors' strengths and weaknesses?

_____
_____
_____
_____
_____
_____
_____
_____

What are your strategies for taking advantage of their weaknesses?

_____
_____
_____
_____
_____
_____
_____
_____

Approximately how much market share do each of your competitors have?

_____
_____
_____
_____
_____
_____
_____
_____
_____
_____

How long have they been in business?

_____
_____
_____
_____
_____
_____
_____
_____
_____

What are their marketing strategies that seem to be working?

_____
_____
_____
_____
_____
_____
_____
_____
_____
_____

What is the diversity of their marketing mix?

_____

_____

_____

_____

_____

_____

_____

_____

_____

What is the diversity of their product and service mix?

_____

_____

_____

_____

_____

_____

_____

_____

_____

What deals have you lost to your competitors?

_____

_____

_____

_____

_____

_____

_____

_____

_____

# Chapter 8

# Marketing and Sales Strategies

*Knowledge is a treasure but practice is the key to it.*
—Thomas Fuller

▶ **Build a great marketing plan**

▶ **Selling tactics**

▶ **Flaunt your Unique Selling Proposition**

▶ **Establish marketing objectives**

▶ **Establish advertising and promotion concepts**

We have all seen great businesses with a superior location and a unique product go broke and close their doors. In most cases, this problem can be traced to poor marketing and promotion. In other words, the owner of the business did not know how to effectively market his or her products and services.

# Build a Great Marketing Plan

Many business owners ignore the great potential of an effective advertising campaign for their quality product. Small business owners tend to overlook this need for exposure. There are four essential areas to investigate:

1. Publicity
2. Promotion
3. Merchandising
4. Market research

Each of these four marketing areas is available to you if you are willing to do the investigative groundwork.

The first step is to define your market. Who is your targeted audience? Know its inclinations, its needs, and its disposition, then gear your product to fit these. Feel free to define it below:

_____

_____

_____

_____

_____

*Entrepreneur* magazine gives us good advice in this area: "All you have to do is forget that you are selling your product or service, and put yourself in your customer's place." Also, it suggests that you ask yourself questions, such as:

- Where do I go to buy it?
- What makes me buy it?
- What media do I watch, read, and listen to that makes me decide to buy?

Simply put, you must know what media your market is drawn to. You must develop a rock-solid marketing plan. Your profits will literally rise or fall on the basis of how well you develop and implement your marketing plan. Here is your chance to show your entrepreneurial expertise. Carefully consider the following ideas and strategies and implement each one into your plan:

- Develop marketing strategies by acquiring market information, by implementing feasibility testing, by accessing competitor track records, and by generating insight into the market's future.
- Pricing a product or service is as much a decision based on customer acceptance as it is on cost. Consumer research and competitor track record and pricing, customer acceptance, etc., should be demonstrated as your basis. In simple terms, charge what the market will bear.
- Determine if your product or service is right for your target market and if they are ready to accept it.
- Channels of distribution need to be effectively and efficiently established if you are going to get your products and services out into the market. This includes production, transportation, materials handling, and product packaging.
- Promote your product or service to your target market. Include the media you will use to promote your enterprise, related costs, and anticipated benefits.
- Your marketing budget must be realistic and clearly communicated.
- Your timetable needs to be accurate and plausible.

## QUICK Tip

Use Complaints to Your Advantage: Look at gripes first, then create a marketing strategy. Look at everything about your industry that could frustrate or irritate a potential customer. Ask people what irritates them. Try to internalize the same problems so that you may experience your customer's frustrations. Then, design your marketing strategy (and even refine your product or service) based on your strengths vis-à-vis these issues.

- Warranty and/or guarantee policies need to be defined.
- Consider what professional resources you need to implement your plan.
- Consider how you will monitor the response of the market to your campaign.
- Testing one approach alongside another will provide direction for future plans.

## Selling Tactics

Identify your sales force. Clearly think through the advantages and disadvantages of commissioned versus salaried sales people. You may consider offering a combination of base plus commissions (monthly salary and car allowance), bonuses, and health insurance. Identify all these parameters in this section.

In the initial stages of your business, will you personally need to go out into the market and promote your product/service? What type of training will you offer for sales staff? Identify the need to increase sales staff as part of expansion and analyze the nature of future staffing.

Will you hire only sales people who have a college degree?

_____

_____

_____

_____

Do your sales personnel need to be licensed by a state regulatory agency?

_____

_____

_____

_____

Will you be selling your products/services through a network of dealers or distributors?

_____

_____

_____

Will your salespeople have protected territories?

_____

_____

_____

_____

_____

Where are these protected territories?

_____

_____

_____

_____

_____

Are your pricing policies set to market or industry standards?

_____

_____

_____

_____

_____

**Cost of Sales:** Many beginners miscalculate the cost of actually selling their product. Entrepreneurs are often very concerned with developing the product to fit a projected need in the marketplace, but forget to calculate in the cost of delivering on that product. Remember to ask yourself: What is the total cost of the sale? How much will it cost me to generate these sales?

Will your salespeople be able to compete with the prices that you have established?

_____

_____

_____

_____

_____

# Flaunt Your Unique Selling Proposition

Don't forget that your Unique Selling Proposition is what clearly sets you apart from your competitors and attracts consumers. Use these questions to help develop your USP.

Will your product or service make your customers' lives more comfortable? How?

_____

_____

_____

_____

Will it save them time or money? How?

_____

_____

_____

_____

Will you offer more customer service than your competition? If so, how is it superior?

_____

_____

_____

Will your customers' lifestyle be any different if they purchase your product/service? How?

_____

_____

_____

_____

_____

_____

Which professional organizations do you belong to that will be of value to your customers?

_____

_____

_____

_____

_____

_____

_____

What are some of your competitors' weaknesses?

_____

_____

_____

_____

_____

_____

How can you take these and turn them into strengths for your enterprise?

_____

_____

_____

_____

_____

_____

## Establish Marketing Objectives

Establish objectives for your next marketing campaign. To help meet these objectives, you should consider four critical goals:

1. To increase brand awareness by a specific percentage
2. To generate high-quality leads for your sales force
3. To improve the morale of your direct sales force
4. To increase sales by a specific percentage within a certain time frame

Once your marketing campaign is underway, begin tracking results. Conduct a few preliminary studies a few weeks into the campaign to measure the results, but don't expect these results to be final. In most cases, you should give your campaign at least twelve months to realize final results. Your target expectations may be realized sooner, which would be the result of a well-planned and well-executed marketing strategy.

## Establish Advertising and Promotion Concepts

Develop a realistic budget for advertising by allocating about 5 percent of expected annual revenues. See Figure 8.1 on the next page for a list of methods you can consider using to promote your business.

Include a good mixture of promotional matter in your advertising campaign. If your budget is relatively small ($100 to $200 per month), definitely include business cards, letterhead, envelopes, a brochure, and stamps. These will give your business plenty of exposure if you carefully follow up on literature sent out.

As you scan the Yellow Pages, you will be pleasantly surprised at the number of organizations you probably never knew existed. Also, consider the various reference sources available in the library.

Clearly define the costs of promoting and holding your own seminar. Include costs for the room, beverages, overhead projectors, writing boards, tables, chairs, microphones, pens and paper, and your printed material.

Next, decide how much to charge for the seminar, or if it should be free. Take into consideration the cost of materials, audiovisuals, promotional costs, clerical support, transportation, and lodging.

### Figure 8.1: **GET THE WORD OUT**

**There are many different ways to promote your business without spending a lot of money. Do a little research on the associated costs in your area for the following items:**

- Radio advertising on one station during morning drive-time hours (6:00 to 9:00 a.m.)

- The cost of a convention hall, hotel, auditorium, gymnasium, classroom, library, etc., that holds thirty to fifty people for a potential seminar

- How much would a live, on-site remote radio campaign cost? This type of investment will bring you hundreds if not thousands of customers within a six-hour time frame, which would justify the cost.

- Have you researched how effective a press release can be for your business? If an editor of a newspaper or a producer of a radio or television show likes your idea, they will do an interview about you and your product or service.

- Look in the Yellow Pages under Television Stations, Radio Stations, Newspapers, and Magazines for telephone numbers. Ask for the name of the business editor or producer. Send them a personalized press release that is one to two pages in length. Follow up in two weeks to find out if they received your material.

- A newsletter is another inexpensive way to gain needed exposure. You could charge for a subscription or send it out free each month or every quarter to existing, new, and prospective customers.

- T-shirts, pens, coffee mugs, paperweights, hats, and the like are a relatively inexpensive way to advertise your business. Check the costs by interviewing several advertising specialty companies and include this in your business plan.

- Offer to give public speeches to several different organizations. The speaking and seminar business will enable you to develop new business relationships. Some organizations to choose from are: business and trade organizations, civic groups, convention planners, service organizers, business firms and organizations, political affiliations, fraternal organizations, athletic clubs, and professional associations.

# Chapter 9

# Management Section

*Real leaders are ordinary people with extraordinary determinations.*
—John Seaman Garns

- **Chart your formal organization**
- **Incorporate your management team**
- **People and talent requirements**
- **Compensation**
- **Directors**

Your management team will be responsible for the success or failure of your business. As you develop your management team, keep this in mind: potential lenders and investment groups will only finance a company with a management team that has balance and the ability to provide the four essential elements of management:

1. Planning
2. Organization
3. Control
4. Leadership

As you write this section of your plan, put down who will be in charge of certain responsibilities and tasks and why they are qualified to manage this specific department or task within your company. Try to keep some kind of balance in your management team. As a whole, this team must have the personal, technical, and conceptual skills applicable to both the production and delivery of your product or service. Skills in marketing, finance, and operations are essential in creating an effective management team.

The strength of your management team must be strongly stated in your business plan. An organization with a formal structure is better able to raise capital, provide leadership, and achieve its goals. When such structure is put in place first, your future goals are easier to achieve with less cost and waste of time.

Review Figure 9.1 on the following page and mentally review your proposed or existing management team. Use honesty in judging yourself and each member of the team. Do not let the "he is a nice guy" or "he never misses a day's work" syndrome sway truth from reality. Always choose the personnel that will drive your company to successful heights. Complete Figure 9.1 for each key management team member.

## Chart Your Formal Organization

After completing Figure 9.1 for each manager, begin to develop a formal organizational flow chart. Keep in mind the structure and size of your organization. It is reasonable for small- to medium-sized businesses to have a management team consisting of one (or possibly two) key management personnel.

## Figure 9.1: **MANAGEMENT REVIEW FORM**

Department of Manager _____

Name of Manager _____

| **Skills** | **Grade** | **Grading Key** |
|---|---|---|
| Conceptual | ☐ | 1=Exceptional |
| Technical | ☐ | 2=Good |
| People | ☐ | 3=Average |
| | | 4=Should not be manager |

Describe strengths of manager:

Describe weaknesses of manager:

Overall grade (see key above):

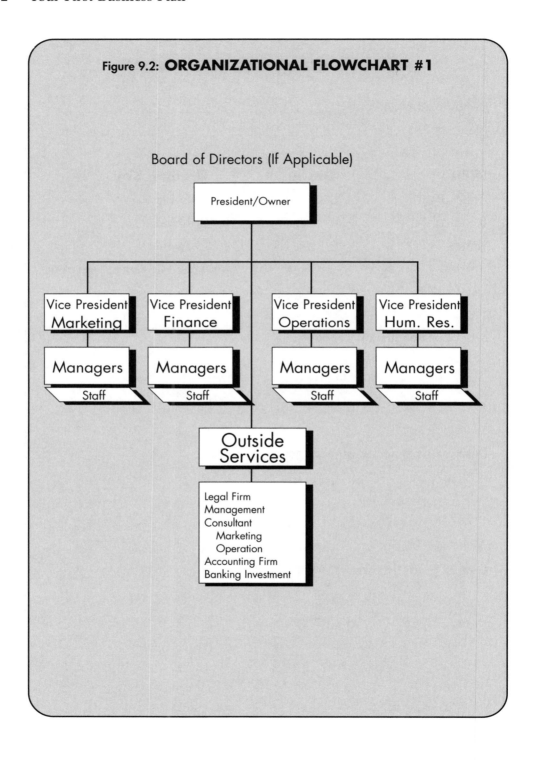

Figure 9.2: **ORGANIZATIONAL FLOWCHART #1**

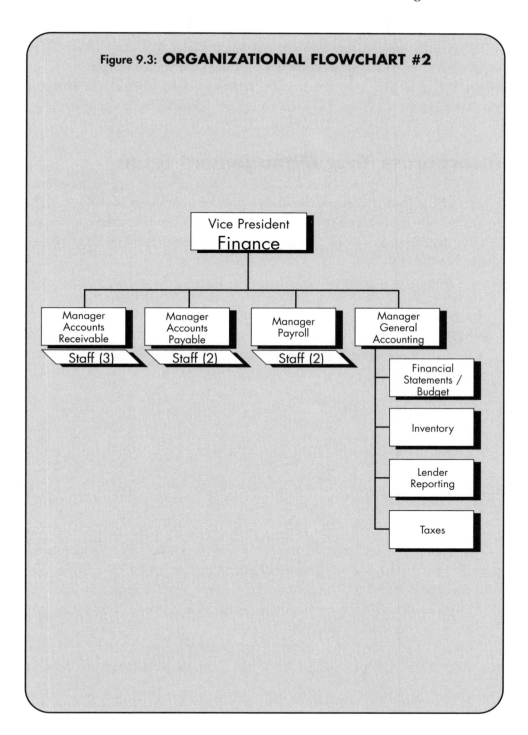

Figure 9.3: **ORGANIZATIONAL FLOWCHART #2**

We strongly suggest that you use outside consultants and professionals to supply any missing expertise necessary to strengthen your management team. Figure 9.2 (page 72) provides a useful example of an overall organizational structure. Figure 9.3 (page 73) shows a further breakdown by department.

## Incorporate Your Management Team

At this point, you have identified the abilities of your key management team and the formal organizational structure of your company. Now, in the final step, you must blend the two together to see if each key function within your organization can be met by at least one team member. Examples of major functions include:

- Marketing
- Advertising
- Sales
- Finance-Controller/Treasurer
- Inventory Control
- Purchasing
- Operations
- Production
- Distribution
- Receiving
- Human Resources
- Legal

Use Figure 9.4 on page 76 to incorporate key management personnel with key functions. For any responsibilities that cannot be covered by current management, check the column for outside services required. You may want to consider contacting outside consultants and professionals who specialize in these areas to assist you.

Now that you have determined your management structure and who should be a part of your management team, begin the documentation process.

## Management

Describe why and by whom the company was started.

_____

_____

_____

_____

_____

_____

_____

_____

_____

## Management Team

The following positions will likely be part of your management team. List the key players, adding positions if necessary.

1. _____president
2. _____vice president
3. _____controller
4. _____marketing manager
5. _____operations manager

Explain their combined experiences, strengths, leadership abilities, and all positive characteristics.

_____

_____

_____

_____

_____

_____

_____

_____

## Figure 9.4: INCORPORATE KEY MANAGEMENT

| Managers / Key Functions | | | | | Outside Services Needed |
|---|---|---|---|---|---|
| | | | | | |
| | | | | | |
| | | | | | |
| | | | | | |
| | | | | | |
| | | | | | |
| | | | | | |
| | | | | | |
| | | | | | |
| | | | | | |
| | | | | | |
| | | | | | |
| | | | | | |
| | | | | | |
| | | | | | |

## Responsibilities

List each manager separately and explain his or her various responsibilities. As you are listing responsibilities, try to determine if any are handling too much—or too little. Would some tasks be better delegated to or handled by other personnel? Be honest with yourself here. Remember, your honesty in these decisions will affect the bottom line of your company.

## Outside Support

Include any outside professional consultant and industry expert who provides support for your management team.

1. Attorney: _____
2. Certified public accountant: _____
3. Business and management consultant: _____
4. Marketing consultant: _____
5. Computer consultant: _____
6. Temporary agency: _____
7. Insurance agent: _____

## Management Résumés

Be sure to provide a brief yet comprehensive résumé of the qualifications of each manager. Include references for key managers.

# People and Talent Requirements

List current and future needs of required company staff. Estimate the number of employees as well as positions needed to effectively operate the business.

_____
_____
_____
_____
_____
_____
_____
_____

## Compensation

List salary histories, proposed salaries, and other compensation for each management team member. Be sure to include bonuses, profit-sharing plans, and other compensation arrangements.

If you currently have or plan to have a stock option plan, be sure to describe it.

_____

_____

_____

_____

_____

_____

## Directors

Provide a complete list of directors. Be sure to include their name, professional credentials, and any compensation you are providing them.

_____

_____

_____

_____

_____

# Chapter 10

# Financial Projections

*In the field of observation, chance only favors minds which are prepared.*
—Louis Pasteur

- ▶ **More than just dollars and cents**
- ▶ **Your financial management tool**
- ▶ **Determining your numbers**
- ▶ **Financial projections**
- ▶ **Implementation schedule**
- ▶ **Statement of resource needs**

For most entrepreneurs, developing an idea or concept is the easy part. Turning it into a profitable reality takes thorough research, especially as it relates to determining the following:

1. Potential markets
2. A realistic selling price for your products and services
3. Assets needed to produce and deliver
4. Costs associated with production
5. Advertising and promotion dollars needed to obtain market share
6. Fixed general and administration costs, including the employee head count, which are necessary to support and operate your enterprise

**Use Proven Numbers:** Every financial claim you present in a business plan should be backed up by quantifiable statistics. If you are a start-up and do not yet have usable sales figures, get them from another source within your industry, cite them, and use them alongside your own projections.

## More Than Just Dollars and Cents

In this section, you should develop a set of financials that will include profit-and-loss statements, balance sheets, and cash-flow statements. A thorough understanding of how they are developed and conceived must be a top priority. Presenting potential lenders or investors with a set of financials is meaningless if they are incomprehensible to you. Therefore, before you dive in and begin crunching numbers, become familiar with financial statements.

If uncertainty exists about your overall knowledge and understanding of financial statements, we suggest you purchase accounting workbooks from a local bookstore, borrow accounting reference books at your local library, take an accounting class at an accredited college or university, or get help from an outside accounting firm familiar with your line of business.

**Use Technology to Good Advantage:**
Modern computers and computer software can be a tremendous help in developing your business plan, especially the financial portions. With the help of computers, you can play "what if" and gain valuable insight into future outcomes based on strategic adjustment variables, such as pricing services in relation to variable costs. Have your accounting experts explain the details, if necessary.

## Your Financial Management Tool

Experience shows that many business owners/managers feel that monthly financial statements are either senseless or useless. This is a big mistake! Financial statements are key management tools, regardless of a company's size or structure. Take the time to learn and interpret what the financial statements are telling you. It could mean the difference between the success or failure of your business.

## Determining Your Numbers

By this stage of the game, whether you are a start-up or existing business, you should fully understand how to project, forecast, estimate, and calculate all items included in your financial statements.

If you need assistance, we suggest you contact a competent accounting firm. It will be able to help you complete this portion of the business plan.

The pro forma schedules shown in the sample business plan in Chapter 13 will aid you in your preparation. The profit-and-loss statement, balance sheet, and cash-flow statement are already completed to help you understand how to produce these statements.

For years one and two, we recommend presenting your profit-and-loss statements on a monthly basis and your balance sheets and cash-flow statements on a quarterly basis. Present years three through five on an annual basis. Examples are presented in the sample business plan in Chapter 13.

**How Software Can Serve You:** Consider purchasing an inexpensive ($60 to $200) business plan software. When it comes to the financial section, business plan software saves you time and energy, and it helps you create a cash-flow budget by using various helpful reports. These reports should compare actual to budgeted income and expenses on a monthly basis.

## Financial Projections

Here is the heart and soul of your business plan, the point in time where your vision is quantified in terms of dollars and cents and units of time (days, weeks, months, and years). Individuals interested in your plan will go through your financial projections with great care. Your financial projections should be broken down into monthly projections for years one and two, and annually thereafter, up to and including year five. If it is imperative to your business plan to include more than five years of financial projections, don't hesitate to do so. Based on this scenario, you should include the following financial statement projections: profit-and-loss statement, balance sheet, and cash-flow statement.

### Profit-and-Loss Statement

The marketing plan you have developed will be used in determining projected revenues over time. Typically, projections become outdated given the impact of all the variables at work in a given enterprise and its market environment. Adjustments will need to be made constantly as you implement midcourse corrections over time.

Next, calculate your cost of goods and/or services sold (COGS), as well as all your anticipated fixed overhead costs. Keep in mind that your COGS will generally fluctuate with revenue volume, while fixed overhead costs will exist on a continued basis.

The net difference of total revenues less total costs will determine the profit or loss of your enterprise.

## Balance Sheet

The balance sheet gives a profile of the worth of your company's assets (cash, accounts receivable, inventory, machinery and equipment, land, and so on) and all the company's liabilities (accounts payable, notes payable, taxes and interest payable, salaries and wages payable, and so on).

The difference between the assets and the liabilities constitutes the net worth of the company (also called owner's equity or stockholder's equity) at any particular moment in time. If you have a track record when the business plan is developed, as in an expansion of an existing operation, then the balance sheet may show considerable equity. If you are starting out with a new venture, the balance sheet may be very simple and show little or negative equity. Work with your local accounting team to develop the details of the balance sheet, if necessary.

## Cash-Flow Statement

The plotting of expected revenues, expenses, assets, liabilities, and equity determines the level of cash flow. Cash-flow totals are a critical index of how successful your business will be. Be sure to identify all changes in detail and leave nothing to the imagination. Be conservative, but realistic.

Please note, as in all number exercises, you should work with your accountant on the details.

### QUICK Tip

Document Your Claims: Where you base projections on specific assumptions (i.e., projections about market response to your goods and services), give evidence that these are based on facts. Assemble and apply expert opinions to substantiate your projections. Use sources such as newspaper and magazine articles, university studies, and interviews of prominent people familiar with your market.

# Implementation Schedule

This portion of the business plan accomplishes the following:

- Identifies when you expect needed financing to kick in

- Lists the main steps of the marketing campaign charted by date
- Gives the scheduled dates of the production and delivery programs that will fulfill the obligations of sales

The implementation schedule enables you to coordinate and manage your enterprise in a systematic and controlled way. This section of your business plan is of critical importance both internally as a management tool and externally as a means of persuading others that you have the smarts to put your project into effect.

**What Comes First?** When preparing your financial projections, remember an important point. When it comes to cash flow, you usually have to pay your suppliers before your customers pay you. This means you have to spend a lot of money before the profits start rolling in. Do the math and plan accordingly well ahead of time.

## Statement of Resource Needs

If you are using your business plan for the purpose of generating needed resources from lenders or investors, this document will summarize your precise needs (capital, terms, requirement date) and identify how the resources will be used.

In the case of financing, your cash-flow projections will, of course, reflect how these funds will be repaid. In the case of capitalization involving equity partners, your projections will give an indication of the growth of equity and the anticipated timetable for the sharing of profits.

## *Statement of Resource Needs*

Our objective, at this time, is to propel the company into a prominent market position. We feel that within five years, HII will be in a suitable position for an initial public offering or profitable acquisition. To accomplish this goal, we have developed a comprehensive plan to intensify and accelerate our marketing activities, product development, services expansion, engineering, distribution, and customer service. To implement our plans, we require a line of credit of $150,000 for the following purposes:

1. Purchase one container of aluminum materials for inventory: $50,000
2. Expand current operations into the rural areas of the United States: $30,000
3. Procure production and computer equipment: $60,000
4. Use as general working capital: $10,000

# Chapter **11**

# Executive Summary

*The last thing one knows is what to put first.*
—Pascal

- First comes last
- Give an overview
- Your statement of purpose
- Your mission statement
- The market, your customers, and your product or service

## First Comes Last

As we have previously stated, the executive summary is that critical portion of an effective business plan, examined first by investors but completed after all other sections have been composed.

Although it comes first in order in a business plan, by preparing the executive summary last, you will be able to write it more easily and with greater impact because you will have already compiled your data in other sections of your plan. Simply transfer the "sizzle" of the plan into concise paragraphs; these paragraphs become your executive summary.

### QUICK Tip

Add Texture to Your Plan: If you hope to secure funding with your business plan, consider using informative and useful visual elements throughout, including charts, graphs, and text boxes to draw attention to important points. Such elements that pop off the page help bring the document to life.

## Give an Overview

Begin by explaining when your company was formed and what you sell, distribute, and manufacture.

_____

_____

_____

_____

_____

## Your Statement of Purpose

Next, explain the purpose of your operation by stating what products/services you will provide your customers; title this the "statement of purpose." Indicate what phase of operation your business is presently in. Show projections that demonstrate how you will cut operating costs by a certain percentage and increase sales by a certain percentage. These two important items will result in a faster return of cash flow to the company.

---

---

---

---

---

## Your Mission Statement

Next, refer to the section dealing with mission statements on pages 4 and 6 and place your own statement here.

---

---

---

---

---

## The Market, Your Customers, and Your Product or Service

Now give some background information on:

- The market

---

---

---

---

- Your customers' buying habits

---

---

---

---

- How you will educate your customers about your product/service

_____
_____
_____

- What type of quality products/services you sell

_____
_____
_____

- Whether or not you will be able to buy from different suppliers at a lower cost

_____
_____
_____

- Who you are buying your supplies from

_____
_____
_____

- How much your operation has produced in annual sales over the past three to five years

_____
_____
_____

- If you have operated at a loss, indicate why and then explain how you will correct this problem.

_____
_____
_____
_____

- List revenue projections for your next fiscal year, and projected annual growth rate (by percentage) for the next five years

_____

_____

_____

Now begin explaining the concept of your products and services. Use comparisons of similar products and services. Indicate any special training required for you or your staff, managers, and sales people to properly manufacture, sell, and distribute your product or service.

_____

_____

_____

_____

_____

Follow this up with whatever strategies you will use to meet the competition. Also, explain the market share you presently enjoy—or will enjoy.

_____

_____

_____

_____

_____

The next step is to clarify your target market. Define your typical customer profile using the information that you wrote earlier in Chapter 3. Also, indicate any additional products you believe your targeted market will respond to favorably.

_____

_____

_____

_____

_____

Next, explain if your products are protected by copyright, trademark, or U.S. patent laws.

_____

_____

_____

_____

_____

Are responses from customers or potential customers favorable?

_____

_____

_____

_____

_____

The next sections of the executive summary are relatively easy because you already compiled the data in other sections. Just give the most important details in a succinct and compelling fashion for the following main sections:

- Objectives
- Management
- Marketing
- Finance

These sections, along with the previous sections, will compile a solid executive summary and give powerful, persuasive information to the reader.

# Chapter 12

# Appendix Section

*Facts that are not frankly faced have a habit of stabbing us in the back.*
—Sir Harold Bowden

▶ **Substantiate your claims**

▶ **Keep it all organized**

## Substantiate Your Claims

The appendix in your business plan should include all of the back-up documents for the data you have already shared. You want to provide as many supporting documents as you can. Two good places to find most of this important information will be the library and your customers.

Your public library carries previously written articles, publications, newsletters, reports, and statistics that will help you verify your claims. Also look for market survey data that has been collected by an independent surveying company.

In the appendix, you also should consider getting letters of reference. Your customers may be your strongest ally when persuading potential investors about your project. If you can persuade loyal, satisfied customers or respected people in the community to write you a letter of recommendation, you will be miles ahead of your competition. Ask them to write this letter on their letterhead.

In this section, also include your brochures, mechanical designs of your product, contracts, media information, and surveys.

## Keep It All Organized

In summary, the appendix section of your business plan might include some or all of the following. Be sure to present this materially in an attractive manner, and organize it logically and coherently. If you need to, add a mini table of contents before your appendix to clearly describe to your reader what it contains.

- Footnotes from the text (assumptions used in projections, further sources of information, and the like)
- Supporting documents
- Articles, clippings, and special reports
- Biographies
- Bibliographies
- Charts and graphs
- Copies of contracts and agreements
- Glossary of terms

- References (lenders, investors, other bankers, or suppliers) who can give positive feedback on your past performance.

※　※　※　※

Congratulations! If you followed the steps in this book, you have compiled a good, solid business plan. Hopefully you have enjoyed the entire process. If we had to bet wages on the outcome of your project, we'd say you now understand your business much better and stand a better chance of achieving your goals. Good luck in all your endeavors!

# Chapter 13

# Sample Business Plan

*Preparing for battle, I have always found that*
*plans are useless, but planning is indispensable.*
—Dwight D. Eisenhower

**Disclaimer**

All information in the sample business plan is fictitious.
Resemblance to an actual company is purely coinci-
dental. It is not intended to compete with any company or divulge proprietary ideas, company structure, or
financial status of any company in any way.

The information presented here is intended to be used
as a guide only. We strongly recommend that the
reader consult with an attorney, accountant, or other
business advisor to verify that the format and structure
is appropriate for his or her circumstances.

# Home Improvements, Inc.

December 2005

Michael X. Swann

President

1234 East Main Street
Suite 1012
Anywhere, Arizona 85999
(602) 555-1919

## Table of Contents

# Executive Summary

In 2002, Home Improvements, Inc. (HII) was formed. During the past year, the company has positioned itself as a leader in the sales and distribution of durable and energy-efficient aluminum siding and double-pane windows.

The purpose of the operation of the company is to provide customers with exterior aluminum siding that is attractive, yet provides a high degree of durability and energy efficiency to home owners and business owners.

Now, HII is at a point where it is entering two separate phases that are projected to cut operating costs by 15 percent and increase sales by 30 percent. By buying direct from the manufacturer, HII will realize better purchasing power and gain hands-on control of the manufacturing and assembly process. This will also cut down on delivery time to the customer, resulting in a faster cash flow to the company.

Our mission statement is as follows:

*To provide customers with high-quality exterior aluminum siding and double-pane windows where we can be proud of the integrity and craftsmanship of each product sold to the end-user, and offer superior customer service throughout the warranty phases of the product, always remembering that each customer may be a tremendous source of referral business to our company.*

## Background

For many years, people have had one of two choices when considering purchasing exterior siding for their home or office:

1. purchase high-quality aluminum siding at a premium price; or
2. settle for a low-quality exterior siding made of wood composite, steel, or low-grade aluminum offered at a lower price.

Potential customers need to be educated on the important fact that all exterior siding is not made the same. When they settle for a lesser quality product, the end results are frustrating and costly.

At HII, we only sell the most highly rated siding on the market today. The company will not sell cheaply manufactured products. However, to accomplish this, HII is currently forced to purchase materials from a single manufacturer. This presents a problem, because HII does not have an alternate source for the product; as well, it is costly to the customer and to HII in potential lost revenue due to higher prices.

As stated, HII is procuring its material as a complete product. Senior management has decided to buy raw material direct from other manufacturers. The product that HII purchases is manufactured in Asia and the United States. These companies have mastered the art of designing and manufacturing aluminum siding through advanced technology. Consequently, the product they provide is superior to any other on the market. Buying direct from the manufacturer will enable HII to save tens of thousands of dollars in the upcoming years, whereby the company can pass these savings on to the customer.

Our operation was producing $200,000 in sales by the end of 2004. This figure is represented by only eight months of operation. These results far exceed industry standards for a start-up enterprise of our size. Projected revenue for the current year ending December 31, 2005 is $320,000.

Revenue projected for calendar year 2006, without external funding, is expected to be $480,000. Annual growth thereafter is projected to be an average of 15 percent per year through 2010.

## Concept

The condition of the industry today is such that people are rapidly becoming aware of the need to protect their assets more than ever before. It has been shown that aluminum siding not only protects your home, but the beauty and attractiveness adds to its value.

Compared to competitive products, our product is made of the highest-quality materials available. There are some companies that sell cheaply manufactured siding made of low-grade aluminum, steel, or wood composites.

The ability to educate customers on the superior quality of our product is a capability unique to our trained salespeople. Each of the company's sales personnel is required to complete a four-week training course before selling to the general public. This is absolutely essential to the success of our business, because of the "value-added" sale. Since our product is made of higher-quality materials, the cost of purchasing the material is higher. Plus, the company is presently buying a finished product direct from a single manufacturer. Once the "middleman" is eliminated, that will no longer be a problem.

Our strategy for meeting the competition is to buy raw material direct from various manufacturers and produce the finished product at HII. This will lower our prices to the customer. Presently, HII has a 30 percent market share in the Arizona market. Implementation of this strategy will result in a 20 percent increase in market share by the end of the first year.

## Target Market

The typical customer profile for the company falls into two separate categories:

1.  households with an annual income of $30,000 to $50,000; and
2.  retired persons in medium- to upper-income housing.

HII is rapidly moving into its third marketing phase, namely expansion of its market base into rural geographical areas, and has relocated to a larger facility in Anywhere, Arizona.

One additional product that HII will provide its customers with is a state-of-the-art rain gutter system that is especially useful in draining water from the perimeter of a customer's house or property.

Another area that will eventually be developed includes an agreement with an Anywhere-based aluminum manufacturing company to supplement parts, thereby lowering shipping costs for some components of the aluminum siding. This will enable HII to purchase components from a local manufacturer.

All products from HII are protected by trademark and copyright laws, and patents from the original manufacturer.

Responses from customers indicate that our current product is enjoying an excellent reputation. Inquiries from prospective customers suggest that there is considerable demand for exterior aluminum siding and double-pane windows. Relationships with leading OEMs (Original Equipment Manufacturers), retailers, major accounts, manufacturers, and distributors substantiate the fitness of the future outlook and potential of the industry.

## Objectives

Our objective, at this time, is to propel the company into a prominent market position. We feel that within five years, HII will be in a suitable condition for an initial public offering or profitable acquisition. To accomplish this goal, we have developed a comprehensive plan to intensify and accelerate our marketing activities, product development, services expansion, engineering, distribution, and customer service. To implement our plans, we require a line of credit of $150,000 for the following purposes:

1. Purchase one container of aluminum materials for inventory—$50,000.
2. Expand current operations into the rural areas of the United States—$30,000.
3. Procurement of production and computer equipment—$60,000.
4. For general working capital—$10,000.

These items will enable HII to maximize sales with an extensive campaign to promote our products and services. It will also reinforce customer-support services to handle the increased demands created by the influx of new orders and deepened penetration into new markets.

## Management

Our management team is comprised of individuals whose backgrounds consist of thirty years of corporate development with major organizations, as well as over twenty-five years of sales and design within the home-improvement industry.

## Marketing

Conservative estimates suggest HII's market share, with our intensified and accelerated marketing plan, product development, manufacturing, and customer service, is about 30 percent (30%) in the Arizona market.

The fundamental thrust of our marketing strategy consists of television, radio, printed advertising, and one-on-one selling in the home. Television and radio advertising have been the most successful marketing methods for HII, compared with flyers, direct mail, and display ads in magazines and newspapers.

We intend to reach prospective clients by continued advertising via television and radio. The marketing promotion tactics will consist of a New Leads Flow System. The customer calls the 1-800 number. The leads are forwarded to HII, whereby HII sends out product information. A subcontracted telemarketing firm calls the original leads and sets appointments for the sales personnel to go on.

None of the competitors of HII are advertising as intensely by television and radio. Our company can be characterized through our marketing efforts as the business that creates a positive and stable image for customers to see.

HII enjoys an established track record of excellent support to our customers. Their expressions of satisfaction and encouragement are numerous, and we intend to continue our advances in the marketplace with more unique and instrumental offers.

## Finance

In twenty-four months, we will have reached our stated goals and objectives and our lending institution will be able to collect its return on investment.

The original loan will be paid down to a balance of zero (as projected in the balance sheet for year three).

# Present Situation

The current situation of the organization is very exciting. We have recently completed a move to a larger and more efficient facility. This move will enable the company to streamline its method of operation and increase its bottom line.

## Market Environment

The marketplace is undergoing tremendous technological change. New technology of exterior aluminum siding is making our product increasingly attractive, stronger, and less costly. We are poised now to take advantage of these changes, and expect to become an important supplier of aluminum siding and double-pane windows.

## Products and Services

The present stage of exterior siding and double-pane windows is the mature stage. This is primarily due to the strong influence of committed manufacturers and the demand for exterior siding.

## Product Life Cycle

Our current product line is primarily manufactured in the United States and Asia. Then it is assembled in Anywhere, Arizona. By buying direct from the manufacturer, HII will cut out 15 percent of our current costs. HII will then be able to pass these savings on to our customers.

## Pricing and Profitability

Current prices are increasing by 10 percent, due to rising labor and material costs in the U.S. and Asian marketplaces.

## Customers

Current customers are using our exterior siding and double-pane windows for added home value, energy savings, storm protection, and noise reduction. They are requesting that we continue promoting our products in their area, so that the value of their neighborhoods will increase, especially during a tough real-estate valuation period.

## Distribution

We currently have one service center in Anywhere, Arizona. Our plans are to open additional offices and distribution centers in Indianapolis, Ind., and Knoxville, Tenn., once the results of operations warrant such centers. Once in place, these centers will reduce freight costs, as well as damage occurring during shipment.

## Management

Most of our management is in place, and HII enjoys a solid managerial staff with many years of experience directly related to the industry.

## Financial Resources

As of November 30, 2005, our current available cash is $22,500. Also as of this date, our Current Ratio is 1.0 and our Quick Ratio is 0.51. Our projected available cash for the years ending December 31, 2006 and 2007 is $36,300 and $11,400 respectfully, while the Current Ratio and Quick Ratio for December 31, 2006, is 5.36 and 1.49, and for December 31, 2007, is 4.74 and 0.86.

# Objectives

The long-term goal of Home Improvements, Inc. is to go public. With the additional capital provided, management intends to expand into rural America and purchase raw material, inventory, and equipment for the manufacturing and assembly of our products. With such an expansive network, we feel we can better serve our target market of middle- to upper-income households and retired persons.

Management also feels that with such a network, they will have stronger buying power and will be able to get more favorable pricing from manufacturers and vendors. This favorable pricing of material and equipment should allow the company to be more price competitive.

The final goal is to become a manufacturer of aluminum siding and maintain the company's distribution and sales operations.

Intermediate goals are to solidify our existing location and bring the company to a more profitable position. Long-term goals call for an 8 percent profit before tax by the end of year five.

In order to achieve these goals, management has set two simple objectives for calendar year 2006. The primary objectives of our organization are:

1. To open up the rural sales offices upon funding
2. To increase advertising spectrum through television and radio
3. To purchase direct from OEMs
4. To begin attending national and international trade shows
5. To hire new personnel and purchase newer equipment
6. To increase training for current and new salespeople

For the company to achieve these immediate goals, the line of credit needs to be structured to long-term debt. This restructuring will better match the terms of the loan with the use of the proceeds. Long-term expansion and restructuring will also significantly improve the cash flow of the company over the next fiscal year.

The industry is expanding and more locations will be needed. Senior management expects to spend the majority of its time and marketing efforts on expanding current and new territories. The required funding is necessary to maintain expected growth. Net profits after tax from sales should approximate a total of $1.5 million over a ten-year period. Total sales for the same period of time are projected to be over $18 million.

### Position for Growth Goals and Objectives

1. Understand customers, competition, and industry
2. Product/service/channel/customer congruency
3. Product/service life cycles
4. Growth by fields of interest
5. Balance people/management/business goals
6. Transition from single-point to distributed management
7. Operate at fifty employees
8. Develop values and culture
9. Hire the best people

We plan to maintain one distribution and service center in Anywhere, AZ, and add two sales and distribution offices and twenty sales-only offices by 2007.

# Management

Home Improvements, Inc. was founded in 2004 by Michael X. Swann, who, after a careful study of the exterior siding industry, found a tremendous void of service and quality products.

This became the principal reason that Mr. Swann wanted to start his own distribution company in the industry. The opportunity to create an entity that offered superior service and products was reflected in his enthusiasm to begin Home Improvements, Inc.

The legal form of Home Improvements, Inc., is an Arizona Corporation. Of the people who make up the development staff, there are several executives who hold the following positions:

- *Michael X. Swann, President*
- *Mary V. Jonstone, Vice President Finance*
- *Roger Armstrong, Director of Marketing*
- *John Herbert, Manager of Production*

The founders and key managers of HII have combined experiences exceeding twenty-five years in the siding and distribution industry.

The strength of the HII management team stems from the combined expertise in both management and sales areas. This has produced outstanding results over the past year.

The leadership and alignment characteristics of HII's management team have resulted in broad and flexible goal-setting to meet the ever-changing demands of the quick-moving marketplace that requires our products. This is evident when the team responds to situations requiring new and innovative capabilities.

## Responsibilities

*Michael X. Swann, President*

Manage market planning, advertising, public relations, sales promotion, merchandising, and facilitating staff services. Identifying new markets, maintaining corporate scope, and market research.Researching and identifying foreign markets.

*Mary V. Jonstone, Vice President Finance*

Management of working capital, including receivables, inventory, cash, and marketable securities. Financial forecasting, including capital budget, cash budget, pro-forma financial statements, external-financing requirements, and financial-condition requirements.

*Roger Armstrong, Director of Marketing*

Manage field sales organization, territories, and quotas. Manage sales office activities, including customer/product support/service.

*John Herbert, Manager of Production*

Service, manufacturing, raw-materials management, and installation.

## Outside Support

An outside Board of Directors, including highly qualified business and industry experts, will assist our management team to make appropriate decisions and take the most effective action. However, they will not be responsible for management decisions.

## Management Team

*Michael X. Swann, President*

Mr. Swann's professional experience includes many different areas in the sales and distribution arena. He has been involved in sales, marketing, and distribution of several services and products for large corporations, such as Big Shoe Stores, Fresh Pine, Inc., and Home Siding 4 You. His experience covers many diverse areas and he has received several awards as the top sales representative for his efforts.

After learning the basic techniques of the siding industry, Mr. Swann worked with the development of sales and distribution for Home Siding 4 You (HSY).

While working for HSY, Mr. Swann was involved with the implementation of a sales and marketing program that increased the company's revenue by 45 percent.

There he enjoyed considerable success as National Sales Manager and Director of Sales and Marketing. However, he became interested in developing a more efficient way to operate a company within the same industry.

With ideas in mind, Mr. Swann conducted a feasibility study to determine the viability of a product capable of competing in the siding industry. When he found that such a market was worthwhile and could be developed, Mr. Swann formed Home Improvements, Inc.

*Mary V. Jonstone, Vice President Finance*

Ms. Jonstone comes from a diverse background in finance and management. She served as a Department Manager for twelve years at VALUE Department Stores and House and Yard, Inc.

Ms. Jonstone has been overseeing the Finance Department for Home Improvements, Inc. since the company's inception.

*Roger Armstrong, Director of Marketing*

Mr. Armstrong's background in sales and marketing has been a big asset to the company. After earning a degree in marketing, Mr. Armstrong went to work as a sales representative for Steel Boxes, Inc. He enjoyed a successful career there.

Mr. Armstrong then moved on to a management position with the multinational corporation Better Products, Inc. As a manager, he was involved with day-to-day operations of inventory control, hiring and training personnel, and developing departmental policies and procedures.

Mr. Armstrong also worked for Top Aluminum for three years, where he earned the Top Sales Representative Award for the entire United States.

Mr. Armstrong has enjoyed a high degree of success at HII. He has helped develop the present sales and marketing structure of the company. As a sales professional, he trains and assists new sales representatives. As a Marketing Manager, he is involved with development of marketing strategies and market research.

*John Herbert, Manager of Production*

Mr. Herbert has a solid ten years of qualified experience specifically in the siding industry. His knowledge of the requirements for proper installation is an important asset to the company.

Mr. Herbert is responsible for several areas related to each project. He oversees everything from the bidding process to the completion of the job, which also includes the timely satisfaction of the customer.

## People/Talent We Require

The HII development team recognizes that additional staff is required to properly support marketing, sales, and research, as well as functions.

Currently, HII is composed of eight personnel. Over the next five years, fifty personnel will be required to meet the demands of the projected market. These staff requirements will include personnel in the following areas:

- Management
- Marketing
- Sales
- Engineering
- Customer Relations
- Administration
- Manufacturing
- Skilled Assembly Labor
- Field Service Technicians

# Product/Service Description

HII products are manufactured in Japan, Korea, Florida, and South Carolina, then assembled in Anywhere, Arizona. State-of-the-art tooling and strict quality-control procedures produce dependable, custom-hardened, aluminum alloy siding.

To fight against weather conditions, each panel is technologically slotted and overlaid on fiberglass insulation of high density. This provides extra insulation value inside the HII siding panel during the entire year.

Trim pieces and eave underpanels are made from extruded aluminum that give the final touches to an attractive product along with securing additional energy efficiency.

The colors available are:

- White
- Cream
- Dark Brown
- Dark Wood Grain
- Beige
- Sky Blue
- Aqua Green
- Sunflower Yellow

Custom colors can be chosen from HII's custom chart, which includes an additional forty colors to choose from. Delivery times for custom colors are usually three weeks longer than for our standard colors.

## Payback

For most customers, HII siding and double-pane windows will pay for themselves in terms of energy savings within twelve years. Research has proved that between 10 percent and 15 percent savings of annual energy costs may be realized by each homeowner. During the hotter months, HII siding and windows intercept solar radiation, thus providing insulation value that allows air conditioners to work about 30 percent less.

In the winter, HII aluminum siding and double-pane windows provide a pleasant insulating blanket. This insulated exterior shield keeps the cold air from entering, and keeps the heat inside the home.

Here are a few of the other outstanding features of HII aluminum siding:

- Premium quality and efficiency
- Lower warranty costs
- Improved energy efficiency
- Improved home value

Even a moment's reflection will prove that personal satisfaction in one's home is worth a fortune. There really isn't a price one could place on the peace of mind that our products give to the home owners. These are some of the nonmonetary benefits of owning HII aluminum siding.

### Useful Purpose and Key Benefits

These combined capabilities provide added value, energy savings, noise abatement, and protection from storms.

This, in turn, can be used to create a sense of greater need in the minds of customers. These are benefits that are worth the extra money and, during our history, have convinced customers to buy from HII.

### Tests

Completed tests have shown that HII aluminum siding has been subjected to many tests of impact by hard and soft objects. These tests are in accordance with the common rules of the Product Durability Testing Requirements set forth by U.S. regulations. The test resulted in a performance that is highly superior to that which the regulations require.

### Product/Service Life Cycle

The life cycle of HII aluminum siding is estimated to be sixty years. The manufacturer's warranty covers all exterior parts for five years.

## Market Analysis

### Market Definition

Currently, the Arizona market distribution is shared by nine participants. Home Improvement, Inc. enjoys approximately 30 percent of this market share. There are four other major competitors that share an approximate 60 percent, and the remaining competitors share a combined total of 10 percent.

The stability of this market segment is expected to increase. However, some volatility has been introduced to the market with the announcement of a national recession.

The exterior aluminum siding market is growing at a rapid rate. The market for siding in the United States is virtually untapped. The United States is a very immature market with tremendous growth potential.*

Over the past three years, companies have developed and shown the additional features that can be provided for this type of industry. These companies have focused on the use of technological advances to steadily improve the quality of aluminum in exterior siding.

The report "New Consumer Product Reports" also states that firms selling home value-added products will prosper greatly in the coming decade.

## Strengths

In marketing, our most powerful assets are the uses of television and radio for advertising and promotion. The public awareness of the HII products and services has been greatly enhanced due to our intense advertising policies.

With a 30 percent market share, HII has the largest share of the market spread among six other competitors. This is not only due to our marketing strategies, but includes our superior customer service.

## Weaknesses

There are some handicaps inherent in our market. The only notable marketplace disadvantages are the prices that customers believe they will have to pay for their home beauty and energy efficiency. Typically, an average job will cost around $13,000, if the entire home is covered with siding and double-pane windows.

Corporate weaknesses, at this time, consist only of not enough sales personnel. However, we are taking steps to interview competent sales professionals, which we feel should alleviate this problem.

There are no environmental threats with our product.

*Source: Westeck, Improved Contracting Unit

## Customers

The person who influences the decision to buy is the stay-at-home parent. They will also permit the purchase to be made. Generally speaking, this is the person who will also choose the color and the areas where the siding will be added to the home.

The most typical customers for our product/service are households earning between $30,000 and $50,000 per year, and retired persons living in middle- to upper-class housing developments.

It is likely that potential customers are going to be familiar with aluminum siding and double-pane windows and that they will readily accept our advertising approach, provided that we educate them in the proper manner. It is also important to point out that our marketing and advertising efforts have been targeted to people concerned about adding value and energy efficiency to their homes, and to retired individuals.

It is easy to understand why the principal buying motives are geared toward our products: because retired persons and housewives are looking for added comfort in and around their homes.

Research indicates that these groups of customers are not as sensitive to pricing differences among competitors. In fact, research also indicates that these people are willing to spend their money on ways that will improve their way of life. It is our task to educate the customer on the superior quality of our products and service.

**Stay-at-home parent**

| | |
|---|---|
| Age: | 35–65 |
| Income: | Fixed |
| Sex: | Female or Male |
| Family: | Full nest |
| Geographic: | Suburban |
| Occupation: | Housewife |
| Attitude: | Security minded |

**Married Couples**

| | |
|---|---|
| Age: | 35–55 |
| Income: | Medium to high |
| Sex: | Male or female |
| Family: | Married or no children |
| Geographic: | Suburban |
| Occupation: | Varies |
| Attitude: | Security minded, energy conscious |

**Older Couple**

| | |
|---|---|
| Age: | 55–75 |
| Income: | High or fixed |
| Sex: | Male or female |
| Family: | Empty nest |
| Geographic: | Suburban |
| Occupation: | White-collar or retired |
| Attitude: | Security minded |

**Elderly**

| | |
|---|---|
| Age: | 70+ |
| Income: | Fixed |
| Sex: | Male or female |
| Family: | Empty nest |
| Geographic: | Suburban |
| Occupation: | Retired |
| Attitude: | Security minded |

## Competition

Competitive threats today come primarily from three major competitors and three other dealers in Arizona.

HII's products perform in virtually all situations where there is a home or office where the siding and windows can be added.

The ability to offer superior beauty, along with full capability to provide an insulating blanket for the home or office, is unique for such an attractive addition to any building or structure.

Our research indicates that the performance of HII's products is superior to anything else on the market today. In all comparisons, the products that HII provides have more features than competitive products, as well as superior performance. In most cases, the number of differences is substantial. A complete technical comparison is available.

## Competitive Products and Services

Companies that compete in the U.S. market are: Home Siding 4 You (HSY), U.S. Aluminum (USA), North East Siding (NES), and Quality Home Products (QHP). All companies mentioned charge competitive prices.

Most of these products do not provide the same capabilities when the construction of the siding is compared to HII's product.

For example, our aluminum siding has been subjected to many trials of impact with hard and soft objects, in accordance with the common rules of the Product Durability Testing Requirements as set forth by U.S. regulations. It turned out to be highly superior to what the regulations require.

## Competitive Roundup

The following chart illustrates how HII compares with the competition in several different key areas.

| | Competition | HII |
|---|---|---|
| Estimated Share of Market (HSY, USA, NES, QHP) | 60% | 30% |
| Rank:1=Weak to 5=Strong | | |
| Product line | 4 | 5 |
| Quality | 4 | 5 |
| Technology | 4 | 5 |
| Advertising effectiveness | 2 | 5 |
| Sales force excellence | 3 | 5 |
| Distribution | 3 | 4 |

| | | |
|---|---|---|
| Seriousness of competition | 3 | 5 |
| Price | 4 | 4 |
| Installation | 4 | 5 |
| Ease of use | 4 | 5 |
| Appearance | 3 | 5 |
| Quality | 3 | 5 |
| Design | 4 | 5 |
| Useful life | 4 | 4 |
| Responsiveness | 3 | 5 |
| Twenty-four-hour availability/support | 1 | 5 |
| Technical expertise | 4 | 5 |
| Repair service | 3 | 5 |
| Efficiency | 3 | 5 |
| Guarantee/warranty | 5 | 5 |
| On-time capability | 4 | 5 |
| Upgrades | 4 | 4 |
| Standing in industry | 3 | 5 |

## Observations and Conclusions

It appears from the above information that some of our competition is faring well in this tough market. However, it is clearly apparent that HII is offering a superior product and service at a competitive price.

# Marketing Strategy

HII's marketing strategy is to enhance, promote, and support the fact that our products/services are superior to others in the market.

## Comprehensive Plan

The overall marketing plan for our product is based on the following fundamentals:

1.  The segment of the market(s) planned to reach
2.  Distribution channels to be used in order to reach market segment: television, radio, sales representatives, and mail order
3.  Share of the market expected to capture over a fixed period of time

To prove the value of exterior aluminum siding and double-pane windows, we will demonstrate two areas that sell our products: added value and energy efficiency. These two areas are a great concern to the customers who purchase our products.

The lack of exterior aluminum siding and double-pane windows in everyday situations is demonstrated by the numerous studies on neighborhood values and energy efficiency.

Because our product is constructed with a high-grade aluminum and installed over superior insulation, an extra value is added to the home year-round. Based on an actual comparison, our product saves an average of 10–15 percent in energy costs.*

## Product Strategy

Exterior aluminum siding and double-pane windows should be treated as a long-term product. The consumer can recoup their investment within the term of a thirty-year mortgage, if one only considers energy savings. However, if one considers the added value of property, the amount of return on investment is immeasurable.

## Positioning

Our products are seen by consumers as ones that protect their homes, as well as protect their pocketbooks, through energy savings.

Their unique advantages can be exploited to arrive at a winning position in the consumer's mind.

*Source: County Gas & Electric

In terms of market segmentation advantages, we can use these factors already mentioned to arrive at a winning position.

By repositioning our product from a cost to an investment in the home, and as an overall attractively appealing package, exterior aluminum siding and double-pane windows become a smart investment for any consumer.

## Outside Suppliers

HII is presently using the firm Superior Media Marketing for the overall television and radio marketing strategy. This has been a good relationship that has lasted since the inception of the company. Superior Media Marketing has the buying power, technical expertise, and marketing expertise that is necessary for a successful campaign. HII is also working closely with TRICO Business Solutions for additional marketing consulting.

## Marketing Responsibilities

The President of HII, Mr. Swann, will be responsible for these marketing decisions:

- New business development
- Dealer and OEM support
- Sales generation tools
- Corporate graphics standard
- Brandmark recognition
- Direct response promotion
- Telemarketing scripts/training
- Product position and identification
- Selling tactics (Refer to section on Selling Tactics for details)
- Advertising and promotion (Refer to section on Advertising and Promotion for details)

## Includes
- Company positioning (identity) within market:
    1. Consistent identity throughout all areas of communication
- Promotional tools:
    1. Brochures and catalogs
    2. Other collateral materials
- Advertising:
    1. Targeted advertisements
    2. Media selection and strategy
- Sales support:
    1. Distributor and retailer support packages
    2. Representative support (sales tools)
    3. Communication within channels of distribution

## Feedback loops
- Lead generation
- Lead referral and follow-up systems
- Information gathering and dissemination

## Strategy Review
Based on the Marketing Strategies, Advertising and Promotion, and Selling Tactics sections, the following questions have been reviewed and answered:

- Do the strategies define means for achieving the objectives management sets?
- Are the strategies consistent with our evaluation of the marketplace and our capabilities?
- Is the return on investment sufficient to justify the risks?
- What are the chances of a competitor executing a similar strategy? In that case, what would happen?
- Have we made sure our strategies are based on facts, and not assumptions?

- Does the overall strategy leave you critically vulnerable to a shift in market behavior?
- Is our appraisal of the competition open-minded and honest?
- Is our strategy legal?
- Is the success of our strategy based on our ability window? What are the chances of failure?
- Have we thoroughly examined alternative strategies? Do we have a sound, deductive rationale for our recommendations?

## Advertising and Promotion

Home Improvements, Inc. (HII) recognizes that the key to success at this time requires extensive promotion. This must be done aggressively and on a wide scale. To accomplish sales goals, HII will require an extremely capable advertising agency and public-relations firm.

The company plans to do most of its advertising on television and radio, in major metropolitan cities.

Once an agency selection is made, its assistance in developing a comprehensive advertising and promotion plan will be needed. Advertising will be done independently and cooperatively with distributors, OEMs, retailers, and companies with whom HII has joint marketing/sales relationships.

## Advertising and Promotion Objectives

The primary reason for such a heavy advertising campaign is to position HII as the leading supplier of exterior aluminum siding and double-pane windows in the U.S. market.

By so doing, HII plans to generate qualified sales leads for field sales representatives, who will be able to take faster action in closing sales. This will be accomplished by cutting out 80 percent of their time directly involved with prospecting. HII's experience has been that sales representatives can optimize the impact of their time by using a promotional campaign like the one that will be used to generate leads.

## Media Objectives

The objectives that HII will obtain with a television and radio advertising campaign will give the company greater public awareness. Television and radio advertising will establish an image of HII as a solid organization that is very professional, completely reliable, and highly visible in the market. This is in addition to the fact that HII has maximized efficiency in selection and scheduling of sales representatives' time.

## Media Strategy

It is the aim of senior management to position HII in select primary publications, radio stations, and television stations with high specific market penetration. Therefore, it is important to schedule adequate frequency to impact the market with a positive corporate image and superior products and services.

Plans are to work closely with a reputable advertising agency to maximize ad life with monthly and weekly exposure of the advertisements.

To get the most out of our promotional budget, the media coverage will focus on two targeted audiences:

1.  households concerned about home value and energy efficiency; and
2.  retired individuals in high-income areas.

An advertising campaign will be built around the added value and energy efficiency of our product, beginning with a "who we are" position and supporting it with ads that reinforce the added value and energy-efficiency message. It is important that a consistent message and frequency be maintained throughout the year.

## Advertising Campaign

The best way to reach our potential customers is to develop an intense advertising campaign promoting the company's basic premise—"Value you can count on!"

To maintain our stable image, the delivery and tone of promotional statements will be based on hard-driving reality that creates a sense of urgency to protect one's assets and energy savings.

Ads will convey the look and feel of a home that is attractive, comfortable, and energy efficient.

Research indicates that television and radio advertising is not heavily used by any of our competitors. The consumer mind-set is that they are eager to purchase a product that will offer a solution to possibly diminishing property values that their neighborhoods may be facing.

Ideally, after becoming familiar with our product and service(s), consumers will be able to take action by calling a toll-free number to place their order, or request that additional information be sent to them, or set up an appointment with a sales representative.

To eliminate the biggest objections to immediate action, the advertisements must address known and anticipated objections, such as How much is their property worth?

Because HII's product is so unique, it is important to develop a promotional campaign that is consistent and easy to understand.

Accordingly, HII has created a system of research and response to ensure the maximum benefit of its advertising dollars. One way to measure the effectiveness of its advertising is to count the number of responses and purchases per one hundred customers given a particular ad.

Research shows that television commercials will bring in an average of forty-eight leads per day. Further research indicates that for every one hundred phone-in leads, the following results are typical:

- 29%   Are not really interested at this time
- 18%   Do not own their home, or are not interested in buying aluminum siding for their future home
- 3%   Give incorrect information (i.e., wrong phone number)
- 10%   Request that we call at a later date
- 40%   Turn into an actual appointment

From the 40 percent, research indicates that approximately 20 percent, or one in every five appointments, turns into a sale.*

## Preliminary Media Schedule

|  | Customers | Budget |
|---|---|---|
| Projected sales (per month) | 15 | $105,000 |
| Monthly cost of advertising |  | $25,000 |
| Anticipated Profits (per month) |  | $8,000 |

We expect to reach a total monthly audience of ten million potential customers.

## Promotion

In addition to standard advertising practices, HII will gain considerable recognition through these additional promotional mediums:

- Trade programs that are offered throughout the Southwest and Northwest Regions
- Press releases sent to major radio stations, newspapers, and magazines
- Radio advertising on secondary stations

The number of trade shows attended will be increased from two to five each year. These shows will be attended both independently and with companies with which HII has joint marketing/sales or OEM agreements.

Reports and papers will be published for trade journals and technical conferences. These reports will be written by an outside consulting agency and edited by senior management.

## Incentives

As an extra incentive for customers to remember HII's name and the service that HII provides, plans are to distribute coffee mugs, hats, and T-shirts

*Source: Marketing Survey Source, Inc.

with the company logo and slogan. This will be a gratis service that will be provided to keep the name in front of customers.

## Direct Mail

In the past, the company has used direct mail as a marketing avenue to generate leads. The type of direct response piece was a house-to-house coupon mailer. This campaign did not generate the responses hoped for.

Senior management was presented with ideas of new plans to refocus direct mail efforts in the form of personal letters, with a detachable return voucher. Research has proved that this is a more effective way of reaching our targeted markets, with a greater success ratio.

## Corporate Capabilities Brochure

Objective: to portray HII as the leading supplier of state-of-the-art exterior aluminum siding.

Recommended contents: use the current corporate brochure with minor revisions to the first page, displaying new management, sales personnel, and our new facilities.

Management: with the new brochure, a portrayal of dedicated, experienced, and professional managers is important in order to depict a team that will ensure complete satisfaction.

Sales: portray HII's full selling team, including representatives and distributors, as a savvy, dedicated support group with one overriding mission: customer satisfaction.

Marketing: present the marketing department in its role of market research, product development, new product management, etc., providing improved product ideas to the user.

## Sales Support Collateral Materials

An additional form of advertising in the home will be used by each sales representative. Each will carry a Video Introduction Tape and give a home presentation. The video tape will be designed to give an accurate description of all the benefits of having exterior aluminum siding. It will enable sales representatives to close more sales, as well as attract new distributors.

In addition, each sales representative will carry a presentation binder that is organized in a "flip chart" format to keep their thoughts in a unified and easy-to-understand style.

The following is a list of items that will assist sales representatives with the communications process during their sales presentations:

- Ads
- Brochures
- Business Cards
- Catalogs
- Charts
- Data Sheets
- Direct Mail
- Resumes
- Handouts
- Videos
- Newsletters
- Post Cards
- Price Lists
- Promotions
- Proposals
- Questionnaires
- Reports
- Stationery
- Telephone Scripts
- Letters

## Investment in Advertising and Promotion

For the first twelve months of the project, advertising and promotion will require $57,600. On a regular basis, HII feels that it can budget its advertising investment at 15 percent of total sales.

This figure is necessary because of the specific goals HII plans to meet. Industry averages for dollars spent on advertising and promotion are considerably less, because competitors are not using television and radio as a marketing tool.

# Selling Tactics

## Current Selling Methods

HII's marketing strategy incorporates plans to sell its line of products/services through several channels:

- Executive selling
- Direct sales force
- Distributors
- Mail-order/direct response
- Telemarketing
- Joint marketing relationships

## Executive Sales

Because our customers tend to be overly conscientious about spending large amounts of money, it is important that our company president and senior managers present our product and service to our customers on occasion.

## Direct Sales

The majority of sales will be through direct sales by the HII sales staff. HII anticipates hiring ten additional sales representatives to cover additional territories and markets to sell specific products.

We have chosen to use a direct sales force because our products require considerable customer education and postsales support directly from the company. Our price point, pricing structure, and profits are such that our cost of sales warrants that sales be handled on an individual basis in this manner.

## Distributors

One of the key elements designed into the HII marketing plan is the targeting of its distributors. It is important to select distribution channels already in existence and staffed with professionals possessing appropriate backgrounds and clientele.

HII products are pertinent to the nature of the distributor's business and to the well-being of its customer base. Also, it is significantly less difficult for us to reach distributors and educate them as to the benefits available in using exterior aluminum siding.

This strategic marketing approach takes full advantage of the tremendous momentum inherent in the fact that these professionals are already involved with parallel products and services. They already have expertise and have been practicing in their field for a long time.

By operating within these distribution channels in this manner, we feel that we can maintain control of our market. In addition, we can generate growth at a reasonable pace and obtain excellent sales results.

- See Distribution section for detailed plan of action.
- See also Advertising and Promotion section on "Direct Mail," regarding appropriate distributors.

## Distribution

HII will use several different distribution channels. The determining factors in choosing these channels are:

- Customer profile
- Geography
- Seasonal concerns
- Efficient use of funds
- Feasibility of using channels of similar products already on the market

## Method

The primary means of distribution will be through company sales representatives. Secondary means of distribution will be through third-party distributors.

An important advantage of these alternate channels is flexibility. By using more than one method, HII will have more control and also more options with which to respond to special needs and circumstances.

Other features of our secondary channels are low cost, quick start-up, increased capacity to reach more customers that are not necessarily influenced by advertising, and promotional methods.

## Coverage

Metropolitan target areas indicate the highest level of consumer interest. Because our distribution network is easy and cost-efficient to implement, we can enjoy delivery almost immediately. This, in turn, will reduce shipping time and increase customer satisfaction. To date, none of our competitors is able to achieve this.

## Roll-Out Program

We have selected from ten key market areas based on proximity—easy to sell into, contact, deliver to, have customers come to, etc.

## Trade Incentives

It is the intention of senior management to offer incentives to regional distributors, such as allowances, co-op accruals, warehouse flushing promotions, etc.

## Customer Service

Our customers emphasize that support is one of their major concerns. They are constantly impressed with the support provided by HII. Hotline service is currently available to all customers enrolled in a maintenance/support program.

We intend to provide free post-sale consultation for customers. The purpose for this service is to ensure customer satisfaction and loyalty and, in addition, allow us to increase sales as well as maintain a high profile within our service area.

Another service to add value is to provide warehousing of customer inventory. This allows us to book larger orders and provide faster order response.

Support to distributors is provided as required. This allows them to perform efficiently as a sales force. We intend to treat the distributors as an extension of the HII direct sales force and they will be given the same support as the HII internal sales staff.

Technical support to marketing and sales functions will be strengthened. Pre- and post-sales situations involving the application, presentation, and demonstration of HII products will be supported by our customer service and marketing staff.

## Returns and Cancellation Policy

At this time, general trade customs for handling cancellations are to provide a full refund of any down payment, if a cancellation occurs within three business days from the signing of the contract.

Refunds are made only on the price of the package, plus applicable taxes, and do not include shipping costs.

Credit card refunds are credited to the customer's account and cash or check payments are refunded within thirty days of receipt of returned merchandise in good condition.

## Business Relationships

HII has formed some very important relationships with major companies in the industry. The following is a list of existing relationships:

## OEM Relationships

OEMs (Original Equipment Manufacturers)—the major advantage of selling through OEMs is to provide a means of more rapidly penetrating the market. Also, these relationships provide HII with national coverage through established sales forces.

We are presently buying from, or developing relationships with, the following OEMs:

1. Craft Aluminum, Inc.
2. All Seal Windows
3. Custom Improvements, Inc.
4. Quality Built Materials
5. Protection Plus, Ltd.

## Joint Marketing Agreements

Joint marketing with established companies will produce revenues, credibility, and market presence.

HII is pursuing joint marketing agreements with other organizations to further the name of our products and services in the U.S. markets. Our plans include having them market our exterior aluminum siding and double-pane windows within their product line.

## Third-Party Supplier Agreements

We feel that we require additional components to enhance the attractiveness of our products and services to customers. Because we do not currently have the resources to procure the exterior aluminum siding from OEMs, we rely on a single manufacturer for the availability of our product line.

# Financial Projections

### Current Assets

1. Cash—reflects limited amount of cash on hand at any balance sheet date. Positive generation of cash is to be applied against outstanding loan. Cash on hand can be eliminated upon implementation of a "direct disbursement" program for both checking and payroll accounts. This will allow Home Improvements, Inc. to maximize the management of cash by borrowing only when required to, and to apply monies received directly against the bank loan payable.

2. Accounts Receivable—are minimal to Home Improvements, Inc.

Company policy dictates cash before installation or approved financing from reputable finance companies on the majority of projects.

3. Inventory—is to be purchased on a container-load basis at a precalculated reorder point determined by lead times provided by the manufacturers. Product on hand will be items already categorized as "work-in-process." Stock available for sale is scheduled to turn over in a six- to eight-week period.

**Fixed Assets**

1. Production and assembly of the aluminum siding requires light machinery. The major piece of equipment required is a twenty-inch radial-arm saw for aluminum cutting. This equipment will be purchased on an as-needed basis with available cash funds.

2. Thirty thousand dollars has been scheduled for 1st quarter 2005 for the purchase of new commercials, new equipment, and office furniture.

3. Depreciation—equipment and furniture have been considered to be either seven-year or five-year property per Modified Accelerated Cost Recovery System (MACRS). Whole-year depreciation has been estimated for all equipment.

**Liabilities**

1. Accounts Payable—includes amounts due on inventory purchases as well as non-inventory items such as supplies, tools, telephone, travel, and entertainment.

2. Taxes Payable—for unpaid Federal, State, FICA, FUTA, SUI, and medical withholding based on current and expected headcount.

## Selling, General, and Administration

1. Officer Wages—for all years have been reflected at market value.

2. Employee Wages—includes all Home Improvements, Inc. employees including sales, general administration, and warehouse. Wage increases for non-officer employees are calculated at 5 percent per annum.

3. General Administration Expenses—have been increased annually by approximately 6 percent to reflect inflationary increases.

## Break-Even Analysis:

Point at which the business neither makes a loss nor a profit.

| Projected for the first month of 2006 | ($ 000) | | |
|---|---|---|---|
| Sales | | | 34 |
| COGS | Materials | 7 | |
| | Labor | 4 | |
| Total COGS | | | 11 |
| Gross profit margin | | | 23 |
| Selling expenses | Commissions | 3 | |
| | Advertising | 4 | |
| Total selling expenses | | | 7 |
| Profit before G&A expenses | | | 16 |
| Total G&A expenses | | | 16 |
| Break-even | | | 0 |

HOME IMPROVEMENTS, INC.
PROFIT & LOSS STATEMENT
YEAR ONE 2006
Rounded to Hundreds ($00)

| | 1 | 2 | 3 | 4 | 5 | 6 | 7 | 8 | 9 | 10 | 11 | 12 | YEAR ONE |
|---|---|---|---|---|---|---|---|---|---|---|---|---|---|
| SALES | 30,0 | 30,0 | 30,0 | 40,0 | 40,0 | 40,0 | 40,0 | 40,0 | 40,0 | 50,0 | 50,0 | 50,0 | 480,0 |
| COGS–MATERIALS | 6,0 | 6,0 | 6,0 | 8,0 | 8,0 | 8,0 | 8,0 | 8,0 | 8,0 | 10,0 | 10,0 | 10,0 | 96,0 |
| LABOR | 3,6 | 3,6 | 3,6 | 4,8 | 4,8 | 4,8 | 4,8 | 4,8 | 4,8 | 6,0 | 6,0 | 6,0 | 57,6 |
| TOTAL COGS | 9,6 | 9,6 | 9,6 | 12,8 | 12,8 | 12,8 | 12,8 | 12,8 | 12,8 | 16,0 | 16,0 | 16,0 | 153,6 |
| GROSS PROFIT/MARGIN | 20,4 | 20,4 | 20,4 | 27,2 | 27,2 | 27,2 | 27,2 | 27,2 | 27,2 | 34,0 | 34,0 | 34,0 | 326,4 |
| SELLING–COMMISSIONS | 3,0 | 3,0 | 3,0 | 4,0 | 4,0 | 4,0 | 4,0 | 4,0 | 4,0 | 5,0 | 5,0 | 5,0 | 48,0 |
| ADVERTISING | 3,6 | 3,6 | 3,6 | 4,8 | 4,8 | 4,8 | 4,8 | 4,8 | 4,8 | 6,0 | 6,0 | 6,0 | 57,6 |
| TOTAL SELLING | 6,6 | 6,6 | 6,6 | 8,8 | 8,8 | 8,8 | 8,8 | 8,8 | 8,8 | 11,0 | 11,0 | 11,0 | 105,6 |
| PROFIT BEFORE G&A | 13,8 | 13,8 | 13,8 | 18,4 | 18,4 | 18,4 | 18,4 | 18,4 | 18,4 | 23,0 | 23,0 | 23,0 | 220,8 |
| TOTAL G&A (SCHEDULE) | 15,7 | 15,7 | 15,7 | 15,8 | 15,8 | 16,1 | 16,1 | 16,1 | 16,1 | 16,2 | 16,2 | 16,2 | 191,4 |
| PROFIT (LOSS) BEFORE TAX | -1,9 | -1,9 | -1,9 | 2,6 | 2,6 | 2,3 | 2,3 | 2,3 | 2,3 | 6,8 | 6,8 | 6,8 | 29,4 |
| ESTIMATED INCOME TAX | | | | | | | | | | | | | 7,4 |
| PROFIT AFTER TAX | | | | | | | | | | | | | 22,0 |

HOME IMPROVEMENTS, INC.
GENERAL & ADMINISTRATIVE EXPENSE
YEAR ONE 2006
Rounded to Hundreds ($00)

| | 1 | 2 | 3 | 4 | 5 | 6 | 7 | 8 | 9 | 10 | 11 | 12 | YEAR ONE |
|---|---|---|---|---|---|---|---|---|---|---|---|---|---|
| SALARIES—EMPLOYEES | 8,8 | 8,8 | 8,8 | 8,8 | 8,8 | 8,8 | 8,8 | 8,8 | 8,8 | 8,8 | 8,8 | 8,8 | 105,6 |
| SALARIES—OFFICERS | 2,0 | 2,0 | 2,0 | 2,0 | 2,0 | 2,0 | 2,0 | 2,0 | 2,0 | 2,0 | 2,0 | 2,0 | 24,0 |
| PAYROLL TAXES/BENEFITS | 1,0 | 1,0 | 1,0 | 1,0 | 1,0 | 1,0 | 1,0 | 1,0 | 1,0 | 1,0 | 1,0 | 1,0 | 12,0 |
| VEHICLE EXPENSE | 3 | 3 | 3 | 3 | 3 | 3 | 3 | 3 | 3 | 3 | 3 | 3 | 3,6 |
| INSURANCE | 2 | 2 | 2 | 2 | 2 | 2 | 2 | 2 | 2 | 2 | 2 | 2 | 2,4 |
| LEGAL & ACCOUNTING | 2 | 2 | 2 | 2 | 2 | 2 | 2 | 2 | 2 | 2 | 2 | 2 | 2,4 |
| GENERAL OFFICE EXP | 1 | 1 | 1 | 1 | 1 | 1 | 2 | 2 | 2 | 2 | 2 | 2 | 1,8 |
| POSTAGE | 1 | 1 | 1 | 1 | 1 | 1 | 2 | 2 | 2 | 2 | 2 | 2 | 1,8 |
| OFFICE SUPPLIES | 2 | 2 | 2 | 2 | 2 | 2 | 3 | 3 | 3 | 3 | 3 | 3 | 3,0 |
| TELEPHONE | 5 | 5 | 5 | 6 | 6 | 6 | 6 | 6 | 6 | 7 | 7 | 7 | 7,2 |
| RENT | 8 | 8 | 8 | 8 | 8 | 8 | 8 | 8 | 8 | 8 | 8 | 8 | 9,6 |
| UTILITIES | 2 | 2 | 2 | 2 | 2 | 2 | 2 | 2 | 2 | 2 | 2 | 2 | 2,4 |
| DEPRECIATION | 9 | 9 | 9 | 9 | 9 | 9 | 9 | 9 | 9 | 9 | 9 | 9 | 10,8 |
| TRAVEL | 2 | 2 | 2 | 2 | 2 | 2 | 2 | 2 | 2 | 2 | 2 | 2 | 2,4 |
| ENTERTAINMENT | 1 | 1 | 1 | 1 | 1 | 1 | 1 | 1 | 1 | 1 | 1 | 1 | 1,2 |
| MISCELLANEOUS | 1 | 1 | 1 | 1 | 1 | 1 | 1 | 1 | 1 | 1 | 1 | 1 | 1,2 |
| TOTAL G&A EXPENSE | 15,7 | 15,7 | 15,7 | 15,8 | 15,8 | 15,8 | 16,1 | 16,1 | 16,1 | 16,2 | 16,2 | 16,2 | 191,4 |

HOME IMPROVEMENTS, INC.
QUARTERLY BALANCE SHEET
YEAR ONE 2006
Rounded to Hundreds ($00)

|  | MARCH | JUNE | SEPT | DEC |
|---|---|---|---|---|
| **ASSETS** | | | | |
| CURRENT ASSETS: | | | | |
| CASH | 52,5 | 45,0 | 38,6 | 36,3 |
| ACCOUNTS RECEIVABLE | 6,0 | 8,0 | 8,0 | 10,0 |
| INVENTORY | 120,0 | 120,0 | 120,0 | 120,0 |
| TOTAL CURRENT ASSETS | 178,5 | 173,0 | 166,6 | 166,3 |
| FIXED ASSETS: | | | | |
| MACHINERY & EQUIPMENT | 30,0 | 30,0 | 30,0 | 30,0 |
| FURNITURE & FIXTURES | 10,0 | 10,0 | 10,0 | 10,0 |
| TOTAL FIXED ASSETS | 40,0 | 40,0 | 40,0 | 40,0 |
| ACCUMULATED DEPRECIATION | 8,2 | 10,9 | 13,6 | 16,3 |
| NET FIXED ASSETS | 31,8 | 29,1 | 26,4 | 23,7 |
| TOTAL ASSETS | 210,3 | 202,1 | 193,0 | 190,0 |
| **LIABILITIES & STKHLDRS EQUITY** | | | | |
| CURRENT LIABILITIES: | | | | |
| ACCOUNTS PAYABLE | 30,0 | 30,0 | 30,0 | 30,0 |
| PAYROLL TAXES PAYABLE | 1,0 | 1,0 | 1,0 | 1,0 |
| TOTAL CURRENT LIABILITIES | 31,0 | 31,0 | 31,0 | 31,0 |
| LONG-TERM LIABILITIES: | | | | |
| LEASES PAYABLE | 20,0 | 19,0 | 18,0 | 17,0 |
| BANK LOAN PAYABLE | 150,0 | 135,0 | 120,0 | 105,0 |
| STOCKHOLDERS' EQUITY: | | | | |
| COMMON STOCK | 10,0 | 10,0 | 10,0 | 10,0 |
| PRIOR YEAR PROFIT (LOSS) | 5,0 | 5,0 | 5,0 | 5,0 |
| CURRENT YEAR PROFIT (LOSS) | -5,7 | 2,1 | 9,0 | 22,0 |
| TOTAL EQUITY | 9,3 | 17,1 | 24,0 | 37,0 |
| TOTAL LIABILITIES & S/E | 210,3 | 202,1 | 193,0 | 190,0 |

HOME IMPROVEMENTS, INC.
CASH-FLOW STATEMENT
YEAR ONE 2006
Rounded to Hundreds ($00)

| | MARCH | JUNE | SEPT | DEC | YEAR ONE |
|---|---|---|---|---|---|
| NET INCOME (LOSS) | -5,7 | 7,8 | 6,9 | 13,0 | 22,0 |
| SOURCE: DEPRECIATION | 2,7 | 2,7 | 2,7 | 2,7 | 10,8 |
| USE: PURCHASE–PROP & EQUIP | 0 | 0 | 0 | 0 | 0 |
| SOURCE (USE) FROM OPERATIONS | -3,0 | 10,5 | 9,6 | 15,7 | 32,8 |
| (INCREASE) DECREASE: | | | | | |
| ACCOUNTS RECEIVABLE | -2,0 | -2,0 | 0 | -2,0 | -6,0 |
| INVENTORY | -95,0 | 0 | 0 | 0 | -95,0 |
| INCREASE (DECREASE): | | | | | |
| ACCOUNTS PAYABLE | -20,0 | 0 | 0 | 0 | -20,0 |
| PAYROLL TAXES PAYABLE | 0 | 0 | 0 | 0 | 0 |
| LEASES PAYABLE | 0 | -1,0 | -1,0 | -1,0 | -3,0 |
| (INCREASE) DECREASE: | | | | | |
| CASH | -30,0 | 7,5 | 6,4 | 2,3 | -13,8 |
| DISTRIBUTION TO STOCKHOLDERS | 0 | 0 | 0 | 0 | 0 |
| CHANGE IN LOAN BALANCE | -150,0 | 15,0 | 15,0 | 15,0 | -105,0 |
| BALANCES BEGINNING OF QTR | 0 | 150,0 | 135,0 | 120,0 | 0 |
| LOAN BALANCE END OF QTR | 150,0 | 135,0 | 120,0 | 105,0 | 105,0 |

HOME IMPROVEMENTS, INC.
PROFIT & LOSS STATEMENT
YEAR TWO 2007
Rounded to Hundreds ($00)

| | 1 | 2 | 3 | 4 | 5 | 6 | 7 | 8 | 9 | 10 | 11 | 12 | YEAR TWO |
|---|---|---|---|---|---|---|---|---|---|---|---|---|---|
| SALES | 70,0 | 70,0 | 70,0 | 80,0 | 80,0 | 80,0 | 100,0 | 100,0 | 100,0 | 110,0 | 110,0 | 110,0 | 1,080,0 |
| COGS-MATERIALS | 14,0 | 14,0 | 14,0 | 16,0 | 16,0 | 16,0 | 20,0 | 20,0 | 20,0 | 22,0 | 22,0 | 22,0 | 216,0 |
| LABOR | 9,1 | 9,1 | 9,1 | 10,4 | 10,4 | 10,4 | 13,0 | 13,0 | 13,0 | 14,3 | 14,3 | 14,3 | 140,4 |
| TOTAL COGS | 23,1 | 23,1 | 23,1 | 26,4 | 26,4 | 26,4 | 33,0 | 33,0 | 33,0 | 36,3 | 36,3 | 36,3 | 356,4 |
| GROSS PROFIT/MARGIN | 46,9 | 46,9 | 46,9 | 53,6 | 53,6 | 53,6 | 67,0 | 67,0 | 67,0 | 73,7 | 73,7 | 73,7 | 723,6 |
| SELLING-COMMISSIONS | 7,0 | 7,0 | 7,0 | 8,0 | 8,0 | 8,0 | 10,0 | 10,0 | 10,0 | 11,0 | 11,0 | 11,0 | 108,0 |
| ADVERTISING | 10,5 | 10,5 | 10,5 | 12,0 | 12,0 | 12,0 | 15,0 | 15,0 | 15,0 | 16,5 | 16,5 | 16,5 | 162,0 |
| TOTAL SELLING | 17,5 | 17,5 | 17,5 | 20,0 | 20,0 | 20,0 | 25,0 | 25,0 | 25,0 | 27,5 | 27,5 | 27,5 | 270,0 |
| PROFIT BEFORE G&A | 29,4 | 29,4 | 29,4 | 33,6 | 33,6 | 33,6 | 42,0 | 42,0 | 42,0 | 46,2 | 46,2 | 46,2 | 453,6 |
| TOTAL G&A (SCHEDULE) | 26,5 | 26,5 | 26,5 | 26,5 | 26,5 | 26,5 | 28,7 | 28,7 | 28,7 | 28,7 | 28,7 | 28,7 | 331,2 |
| PROFIT (LOSS) BEFORE TAX | 2,9 | 2,9 | 2,9 | 7,1 | 7,1 | 13,3 | 13,3 | 13,3 | 13,3 | 17,5 | 17,5 | 17,5 | 122,4 |
| ESTIMATED INCOME TAX | | | | | | | | | | | | | 43,4 |
| PROFIT AFTER TAX | | | | | | | | | | | | | 79,0 |

## HOME IMPROVEMENTS, INC.
## GENERAL & ADMINISTRATIVE EXPENSE
### YEAR TWO 2007
Rounded to Hundreds ($00)

| | 1 | 2 | 3 | 4 | 5 | 6 | 7 | 8 | 9 | 10 | 11 | 12 | YEAR ONE |
|---|---|---|---|---|---|---|---|---|---|---|---|---|---|
| SALARIES—EMPLOYEES | 14,4 | 14,4 | 14,4 | 14,4 | 14,4 | 14,4 | 16,0 | 16,0 | 16,0 | 16,0 | 16,0 | 16,0 | 182,4 |
| SALARIES—OFFICERS | 5,0 | 5,0 | 5,0 | 5,0 | 5,0 | 5,0 | 5,0 | 5,0 | 5,0 | 5,0 | 5,0 | 5,0 | 60,0 |
| PAYROLL TAXES/BENEFITS | 1,6 | 1,6 | 1,6 | 1,6 | 1,6 | 1,6 | 1,7 | 1,7 | 1,7 | 1,7 | 1,7 | 1,7 | 19,8 |
| VEHICLE EXPENSE | 4 | 4 | 4 | 4 | 4 | 4 | 4 | 4 | 4 | 4 | 4 | 4 | 4,8 |
| INSURANCE | 3 | 3 | 3 | 3 | 3 | 3 | 3 | 3 | 3 | 3 | 3 | 3 | 3,6 |
| LEGAL & ACCOUNTING | 3 | 3 | 3 | 3 | 3 | 3 | 3 | 3 | 3 | 3 | 3 | 3 | 3,6 |
| GENERAL OFFICE EXP | 2 | 2 | 2 | 2 | 2 | 2 | 3 | 3 | 3 | 3 | 3 | 3 | 3,0 |
| POSTAGE | 2 | 2 | 2 | 2 | 2 | 2 | 3 | 3 | 3 | 3 | 3 | 3 | 3,0 |
| OFFICE SUPPLIES | 3 | 3 | 3 | 3 | 3 | 3 | 4 | 4 | 4 | 4 | 4 | 4 | 4,2 |
| TELEPHONE | 8 | 8 | 8 | 8 | 8 | 8 | 1,0 | 1,0 | 1,0 | 1,0 | 1,0 | 1,0 | 10,8 |
| RENT | 8 | 8 | 8 | 8 | 8 | 8 | 8 | 8 | 8 | 8 | 8 | 8 | 9,6 |
| UTILITIES | 3 | 3 | 3 | 3 | 3 | 3 | 3 | 3 | 3 | 3 | 3 | 3 | 3,6 |
| DEPRECIATION | 1,2 | 1,2 | 1,2 | 1,2 | 1,2 | 1,2 | 1,2 | 1,2 | 1,2 | 1,2 | 1,2 | 1,2 | 14,4 |
| TRAVEL | 3 | 3 | 3 | 3 | 3 | 3 | 3 | 3 | 3 | 3 | 3 | 3 | 3,6 |
| ENTERTAINMENT | 2 | 2 | 2 | 2 | 2 | 2 | 2 | 2 | 2 | 2 | 2 | 2 | 2,4 |
| MISCELLANEOUS | 2 | 2 | 2 | 2 | 2 | 2 | 2 | 2 | 2 | 2 | 2 | 2 | 2,4 |
| TOTAL G&A EXPENSE | 26,5 | 26,5 | 26,5 | 26,5 | 26,5 | 26,5 | 28,7 | 28,7 | 28,7 | 28,7 | 28,7 | 28,7 | 331,2 |

HOME IMPROVEMENTS, INC.
QUARTERLY BALANCE SHEET
YEAR TWO 2007
Rounded to Hundreds ($00)

|  | MARCH | JUNE | SEPT | DEC |
|---|---|---|---|---|
| **ASSETS** | | | | |
| CURRENT ASSETS: | | | | |
| CASH | 6,2 | 13,1 | 16,7 | 11,4 |
| ACCOUNTS RECEIVABLE | 14,0 | 16,0 | 20,0 | 22,0 |
| INVENTORY | 130,0 | 130,0 | 150,0 | 150,0 |
| TOTAL CURRENT ASSETS | 150,2 | 159,1 | 186,7 | 183,4 |
| FIXED ASSETS: | | | | |
| MACHINERY & EQUIPMENT | 50,0 | 50,0 | 50,0 | 50,0 |
| FURNITURE & FIXTURES | 20,0 | 20,0 | 20,0 | 20,0 |
| TOTAL FIXED ASSETS | 70,0 | 70,0 | 70,0 | 70,0 |
| ACCUMULATED DEPRECIATION | 19,9 | 23,5 | 27,1 | 30,7 |
| NET FIXED ASSETS | 50,1 | 46,5 | 42,9 | 39,3 |
| TOTAL ASSETS | 200,3 | 205,6 | 229,6 | 222,7 |
| **LIABILITIES & STKHLDRS EQUITY** | | | | |
| CURRENT LIABILITIES: | | | | |
| ACCOUNTS PAYABLE | 37,0 | 37,0 | 37,0 | 37,0 |
| PAYROLL TAXES PAYABLE | 1,6 | 1,6 | 1,7 | 1,7 |
| TOTAL CURRENT LIABILITIES | 38,6 | 38,6 | 38,7 | 38,7 |
| LONG-TERM LIABILITIES: | | | | |
| LEASES PAYABLE | 26,0 | 25,0 | 24,0 | 23,0 |
| BANK LOAN PAYABLE | 90,0 | 75,0 | 60,0 | 45,0 |
| STOCKHOLDERS' EQUITY: | | | | |
| COMMON STOCK | 10,0 | 10,0 | 10,0 | 10,0 |
| PRIOR YEAR PROFIT (LOSS) | 27,0 | 27,0 | 27,0 | 27,0 |
| CURRENT YEAR PROFIT (LOSS) | 8,7 | 30,0 | 69,9 | 79,0 |
| TOTAL EQUITY | 45,7 | 67,0 | 106,9 | 116,0 |
| TOTAL LIABILITIES & S/E | 200,3 | 205,6 | 229,6 | 222,7 |

HOME IMPROVEMENTS, INC.
CASH-FLOW STATEMENT
YEAR TWO 2007
Rounded to Hundreds ($00)

| | MARCH | JUNE | SEPT | DEC | YEAR ONE |
|---|---|---|---|---|---|
| NET INCOME (LOSS) | 8,7 | 21,3 | 39,9 | 9,1 | 79,0 |
| SOURCE: DEPRECIATION | 3,6 | 3,6 | 3,6 | 3,6 | 14,4 |
| USE: PURCHASE–PROP & EQUIP | 30,0 | 0 | 0 | 0 | 30,0 |
| SOURCE (USE) FROM OPERATIONS | -17,7 | 24,9 | 43,5 | 12,7 | 63,4 |
| (INCREASE) DECREASE: | | | | | |
| ACCOUNTS RECEIVABLE | -4,0 | -2,0 | -4,0 | -2,0 | -12,0 |
| INVENTORY | -10,0 | 0 | -20,0 | 0 | -30,0 |
| INCREASE (DECREASE): | | | | | |
| ACCOUNTS PAYABLE | 7,0 | 0 | 0 | 0 | 7,0 |
| PAYROLL TAXES PAYABLE | 6 | 0 | 1 | 0 | 7 |
| LEASES PAYABLE | 9,0 | -1,0 | -1,0 | -1,0 | 6,0 |
| (INCREASE) DECREASE: | | | | | |
| CASH | 30,1 | 6,9 | 3,6 | 5,3 | 24,9 |
| DISTRIBUTION TO STOCKHOLDERS | 0 | 0 | 0 | 0 | 0 |
| CHANGE IN LOAN BALANCE | 15,0 | 15,0 | 15,0 | 15,0 | 60,0 |
| BALANCES BEGINNING OF QTR | 105,0 | 90,0 | 75,0 | 60,0 | 105,0 |
| LOAN BALANCE END OF QTR | 90,0 | 75,0 | 60,0 | 45,0 | 45,0 |

HOME IMPROVEMENTS, INC.
PROFIT & LOSS STATEMENT
YEARS THREE TO FIVE
Rounded to Thousands ($000)

| | YEAR THREE | YEAR FOUR | YEAR FIVE |
|---|---|---|---|
| SALES | 1,240 | 1,430 | 1,640 |
| COGS–MATERIALS | 260 | 300 | 350 |
| LABOR | 160 | 190 | 220 |
| TOTAL COGS | 420 | 490 | 570 |
| GROSS PROFIT/MARGIN | 820 | 940 | 1,070 |
| SELLING–COMMISSIONS | 124 | 143 | 164 |
| ADVERTISING | 186 | 215 | 246 |
| TOTAL SELLING | 310 | 358 | 410 |
| PROFIT BEFORE G&A | 510 | 582 | 660 |
| TOTAL G&A (SCHEDULE) | 477 | 505 | 521 |
| PROFIT BEFORE TAX | 33 | 77 | 139 |
| ESTIMATED INCOME TAX | 8 | 20 | 47 |
| PROFIT AFTER TAX | 25 | 57 | 92 |

HOME IMPROVEMENTS, INC.
GENERAL & ADMINISTRATIVE EXPENSE
YEARS THREE TO FIVE
Rounded to Thousands ($000)

| | YEAR THREE | YEAR FOUR | YEAR FIVE |
|---|---|---|---|
| SALARIES—EMPLOYEES | 288 | 294 | 300 |
| SALARIES—OFFICERS | 72 | 78 | 84 |
| PAYROLL TAXES/BENEFITS | 28 | 30 | 31 |
| VEHICLE EXPENSE | 6 | 7 | 7 |
| INSURANCE | 4 | 5 | 5 |
| LEGAL & ACCOUNTING | 6 | 7 | 7 |
| GENERAL OFFICE EXP | 4 | 5 | 5 |
| POSTAGE | 4 | 5 | 5 |
| OFFICE SUPPLIES | 5 | 6 | 6 |
| TELEPHONE | 12 | 13 | 13 |
| RENT | 14 | 14 | 14 |
| UTILITIES | 6 | 7 | 7 |
| DEPRECIATION | 17 | 20 | 23 |
| TRAVEL | 5 | 6 | 6 |
| ENTERTAINMENT | 3 | 4 | 4 |
| MISCELLANEOUS | 3 | 4 | 4 |
| TOTAL G&A EXPENSE | 477 | 505 | 521 |

HOME IMPROVEMENTS, INC.
BALANCE SHEET
YEARS THREE TO FIVE
Rounded to Thousands ($000)

|  | YEAR THREE | YEAR FOUR | YEAR FIVE |
|---|---|---|---|
| **ASSETS** | | | |
| CURRENT ASSETS: | | | |
| CASH | 24 | 71 | 126 |
| ACCOUNTS RECEIVABLE | 25 | 25 | 30 |
| INVENTORY | 150 | 170 | 200 |
| TOTAL CURRENT ASSETS | 199 | 266 | 356 |
| FIXED ASSETS: | | | |
| MACHINERY & EQUIPMENT | 70 | 90 | 110 |
| FURNITURE & FIXTURES | 30 | 40 | 50 |
| TOTAL FIXED ASSETS | 100 | 130 | 160 |
| ACCUMULATED DEPRECIATION | 48 | 68 | 91 |
| NET FIXED ASSETS | 52 | 62 | 69 |
| TOTAL ASSETS | 251 | 328 | 425 |
| **LIABILITIES & STKHLDRS EQUITY** | | | |
| CURRENT LIABILITIES: | | | |
| ACCOUNTS PAYABLE | 65 | 65 | 75 |
| PAYROLL TAXES PAYABLE | 5 | 5 | 5 |
| TOTAL CURRENT LIABILITIES | 70 | 70 | 80 |
| LONG-TERM LIABILITIES: | | | |
| LEASES PAYABLE | 40 | 60 | 55 |
| BANK LOAN PAYABLE | 0 | 0 | 0 |
| STOCKHOLDERS' EQUITY: | | | |
| COMMON STOCK | 10 | 10 | 10 |
| PRIOR YEAR PROFIT | 106 | 131 | 188 |
| CURRENT YEAR PROFIT | 25 | 57 | 92 |
| DISTRIBUTION TO STOCKHOLDERS | 0 | 0 | 0 |
| TOTAL EQUITY | 141 | 198 | 290 |
| TOTAL LIABILITIES & S/E | 251 | 328 | 425 |

HOME IMPROVEMENTS, INC.
CASH-FLOW STATEMENT
YEARS THREE TO FIVE
Rounded to Thousands ($000)

| | YEAR THREE | YEAR FOUR | YEAR FIVE |
|---|---|---|---|
| NET INCOME (LOSS) | 25 | 57 | 92 |
| SOURCE: DEPRECIATION | 17 | 20 | 23 |
| USE: PURCHASE–PROP & EQUIP | 30 | 30 | 30 |
| SOURCE (USE) FROM OPERATIONS | 12 | 47 | 85 |
| (INCREASE) DECREASE: | | | |
| ACCOUNTS RECEIVABLE | -3 | 0 | -5 |
| INVENTORY | 0 | -20 | -30 |
| INCREASE (DECREASE): | | | |
| ACCOUNTS PAYABLE | 28 | 0 | 10 |
| PAYROLL TAXES PAYABLE | 4 | 0 | 0 |
| LEASES PAYABLE | 17 | 20 | -5 |
| (INCREASE) DECREASE: | | | |
| CASH | -13 | -47 | -55 |
| DISTRIBUTION TO STOCKHOLDERS | 0 | 0 | 0 |
| CHANGE IN LOAN BALANCE | 45 | 0 | 0 |
| BALANCES BEGINNING OF QTR | 45 | 0 | 0 |
| LOAN BALANCE END OF QTR | 0 | 0 | 0 |

# Appendix

- Letters of Recommendation
- Market Survey Data
- Television and Radio Advertising Statement
- Property Value and Statistics
- Mechanical Designs of the Product
- Company Brochures

Note: The appendix should include all documentation that will support and add value to your organization. The above outline only covers several examples of items that could be included in the appendix of your business plan.

# Appendix 1

# 101-Plus
# Questions to Success

*No man really becomes a fool until he stops asking questions.*
—Charles Steinmetz

The following checklist will help you create a better overall picture of how to structure your business plan. It is intended to assist you in thinking through the key elements of your enterprise and will give you most of the answers that are needed to write a comprehensive plan.

1.   What is the nature of your business (retailing products to consumers' real estate sales; manufacturing; mail order; etc.)?

_____

_____

_____

2.   What phase is your business in?
   a. Start-up _____
   b. Expansion _____
   c. Cash flow shortage _____
   d. Other _____

3.   What is your corporate structure?
   a. Sole proprietor _____
   b. Partnership _____
   c. Limited partnership _____
   d. Minority-owned _____
   e. Woman-owned _____
   f. Corporation   C Corp. ☐     S Corp. ☐
   g. Not for profit _____
   h. Other _____

4.   Who is your management team?
   a. President _____
   b. Vice president_____
   c. Secretary _____
   d. Treasurer _____
   e. Controller _____
   f. Marketing manager_____
   g. Sales manager _____
   h. Operation manager _____
   i. Human resource manager _____

5.   Who is on your outside consultant team?
   a. Legal_____

b. Management consultant  _____

c. Marketing  _____

d. Accounting _____

e. Computer software  _____

f. Computer hardware  _____

6.    What is your Unique Selling Proposition (USP)? (Give details on why your product/service is unique.)

_____

_____

_____

_____

_____

7.    What are your goals and objectives?

_____

_____

_____

_____

_____

8.    What would you like to achieve in annual sales volume?

a. Year one $  _____

b. Year two $  _____

c. Year five $  _____

d. Year ten $  _____

9.    How do you plan to achieve your annual sales volume goals?

_____

_____

_____

_____

_____

_____

10. What do you want for yourself, both personally and financially?

_____

_____

_____

_____

_____

11. What will you develop?

_____

_____

_____

_____

_____

12. What will you achieve?

_____

_____

_____

_____

_____

13. How will your company fit into the industry?

_____

_____

_____

_____

14. How will your investors receive their return on investment (go public in five years, be acquired in four years, etc.)?

_____

_____

_____

_____

15. What is your customer profile? (Give details on your typical customers.)
    **Business customer**
    Type of business _____
    Size of business (approximate annual revenues) _____
    Geographical area _____
    Number of employees _____
    Years in business_____
    **Individual consumer**
    Age _____
    Income_____
    Sex _____
    Occupation _____
    Family size _____
    Culture _____
    Education _____

16. Who is your competition?
    a. _____
    b. _____
    c. _____
    d. _____
    e. _____
    f. _____
    g. _____
    h. _____

17. How is your competition promoting its product or service?

    _____
    _____
    _____
    _____

18. What are your company plans?
    a. Sales and marketing plans

    _____

_____
_____
_____
_____

b. Technical and engineering

_____
_____
_____
_____
_____

c. Franchise or distributor plans

_____
_____
_____
_____
_____

d. Personnel

_____
_____
_____
_____
_____

19. How much capital do you need for two years of operation?

_____

20. What will the capital be used for?

_____
_____
_____

21. What type of borrowing structure are you looking for?
    a. Debt only _____
    b. Debt/equity_____
    c. Limited partnership _____
    d. Stock purchase _____
    e. Venture capital _____

22.   What type of payback to the lender/investor are you looking for?

_____

_____

23.   What equipment do you need? (Please list type of equipment and retail costs, such as machinery and equipment, furniture and fixtures, vehicles, office machines and equipment, telephone systems.)

_____

_____

_____

_____

_____

24.   What inventory do you need? (List type of inventory you need.)

_____

_____

_____

_____

_____

25.   Will you be leasing office/warehouse space, or purchasing? Give details.

_____

_____

_____

26.   What existing loans do you have?

_____

_____

_____

27.   What will you do with these loans?

_____

_____

_____

28.  Will you/do you have salespeople? If yes, please indicate their territories, commissions, and salary structures.

_____

_____

_____

_____

_____

29.  How many salespeople do you/will you have on staff during the next twenty-four months?
    a. Outside  _____

    b. Inside  _____

30.  What are all your business assets?

_____

_____

_____

31.  What are all your business liabilities?

_____

_____

_____

32.  When does your fiscal year end? _____

33.  What were the past three years' prior results?

|                        | Year One | Year Two | Year Three |
|------------------------|----------|----------|------------|
| Sales                  | _____ | _____ | _____   |
| Cost of sales          | _____ | _____ | _____   |
| (Variable costs)       |          |          |            |
| Gross profit           | _____ | _____ | _____   |
|                        |          |          |            |
| Operating expenses     | _____ | _____ | _____   |
| (Fixed costs)          |          |          |            |
| Profit or loss         | _____ | _____ | _____   |

34. What type of inventory do you have?
    a. FIFO (first in, last out) _____
    b. LIFO (last in, first out) _____

35. How much inventory do you/will you carry in an average month?

    _____
    _____

36. How much in receivables do you carry on average?
    a. 30 days_____
    b. 60 days_____
    c. 90 days_____
    d. 120 days _____
    e. Over 120 days _____
    f. TOTAL _____

37. How will you promote your product or service?

    _____
    _____
    _____
    _____
    _____

38. How much will you spend on advertising in a typical year? (List in dollars and as a percentage of gross revenues.)

    _____
    _____
    _____
    _____

39. Have you defined your market into a narrow window?

    _____
    _____
    _____
    _____

40.  What is your market? (For example, do you market only to the medical profession?)

_____

_____

_____

41.  What is your current and/or anticipated market share over the next five years? (25 percent? 30 percent?) _____

42.  How much working capital will you need?
    a. One year _____
    b. Two years_____

43.  Who are your suppliers?
    1. _____
    2. _____
    3. _____
    4. _____
    5. _____
    6. _____
    7. _____
    8. _____
    9. _____
    10. _____

44.  Do you have
    a. Letters of recommendation?_____
    b. Endorsements? _____
    c. References? _____

45.  Do you have one or two (or more) faithful customers who buy from you on a regular basis? _____

46.  What percentage do they represent of your overall business?_____

47.  Give some background information on the management team (graduated from college, worked for a Fortune 500 Company, increased sales by 50 percent, developed new personnel handbook, and so on).

_____

_____

_____

_____

_____

_____

_____

_____

_____

_____

48.  What is your primary means of distribution (dealers, salespeople, mail order, or something else)?

_____

_____

_____

_____

49.  What are your coverage areas for distribution?

_____

_____

_____

_____

50.  Does your marketing strategy incorporate any of the following?
    a. Executive selling (that is, owners or managers of your company out in the field selling)? _____
    b. Direct sales force? _____
    c. Manufacturer's reps? _____
    d. Distributors? _____

51.  If so, please give some details.

_____

_____

_____

52.  How do you set your prices?

_____

_____

_____

53.  What are your profit margins?

_____

_____

_____

54.  What is your present situation?

_____

_____

_____

55.  Financial Resources:
     Current cash available is:  _____

     Your Current Ratio is:

$$\frac{\text{Current Assets}}{\text{Current Liabilities}} \quad = \quad \underline{\hspace{4cm}}$$

     Your Quick Ratio is:

$$\frac{\text{Cash and Equivalents + Accounts Receivable + Notes Receivable}}{\text{Total Current Liabilities}}$$

$$= \quad \underline{\hspace{3cm}}$$

56.   Are you aware of the Small Business Administration (SBA) procedures for obtaining a loan? _____

57.   What is the precise nature of your business?

_____

_____

_____

58.   Provide a brief history of the business and tell how you develop your products or services.

_____

_____

_____

_____

_____

59.   What are the economic forecasts that indicate spending trends are favorable to your specific industry?

_____

_____

_____

_____

_____

60.   Is your business seasonal?

_____

_____

_____

61.   If yes, how will you maintain cash flow for the slower times of the year?

_____

_____

_____

62.  Do you, or will you, depend on special vendors or suppliers to successfully operate your business?

_____

_____

_____

63.  Do you have any licenses or agreements that are required to operate your business?

_____

_____

_____

64.  How will your product or service differ from similar products or services?

_____

_____

_____

_____

_____

65.  How will you satisfy your customers' needs and wants?

_____

_____

_____

_____

_____

66.  Will your products or services save your customers, time, money, or both? How?

_____

_____

_____

_____

_____

67.   Are there any case studies that have been performed that will help you back up your claims?

_____

_____

_____

68.   What is the life cycle of your product or service?

_____

_____

_____

69.   How many competitors share your market? _____

70.   Who are they and where are they located?

_____

_____

_____

_____

_____

71.   How is the share of the market distributed among the major participants?

_____

_____

_____

_____

_____

72.   What are the strengths of your management team?

_____

_____

_____

_____

_____

73.   What are the strengths of your products or services?

_____

_____

_____

74.   What are the strengths of your marketing plan?

_____

_____

_____

75.   What are some of the weaknesses of your management team?

_____

_____

_____

76.   What are some of the weaknesses of your products or services?

_____

_____

_____

77.   What are some of the weaknesses of your marketing plan?

_____

_____

_____

78.   What advantages do you have over your competition in the following areas:

a. Performance?

_____

_____

_____

b. Quality and reliability?

_____

_____

_____

c. Production efficiencies?

_____

_____

_____

d. Distribution?

_____

_____

_____

e. Pricing?

_____

_____

_____

f. Public image?

_____

_____

_____

g. Business relationships or references?

_____

_____

_____

79. Who or what is your target market?

_____

_____

_____

80. What strategies may be adopted to your environment that your competition is using?

_____

_____

_____

81. How will you promote your products and services (television, radio, seminars, brochures, salespeople, direct mail, etc.)?

_____

_____

_____

_____

82.   What are the associated costs for each area of promotion?

_____

_____

_____

83.   What are the associated frequencies of media coverage?

_____

_____

_____

84.   Who is your management consultant?   _____

85.   Who is your attorney?  _____

86.   Who is your banker?  _____

87.   What type of computers do you need to operate your business?

_____

_____

_____

88.   How many computers do you need?  _____

89.   What kind(s) of software do you need (business management, accounting, word processing, mailing lists, etc.)?

_____

_____

_____

_____

_____

90.   What other equipment do you need to operate your business?

_____

_____

_____

_____

91.  Does your product need to be patented? _____

92.  If so, have you applied for a patent? _____

93.  What is the sales tax rate for each state, city, or county in which you plan to transact business? _____

94.  Do you have a current personal financial statement? _____

95.  When is your business financial statement updated (monthly, quarterly, annually)? _____

96.  What is your break-even point, according to your financial projections?

_____

97.  Does your business have a current profit and loss statement, balance sheet, cash flow statement, and at least two years' financial projections?

_____

98.  What do you have to pledge as collateral (inventory, accounts receivable, fixed assets, stock, other marketable securities, contracts, etc.)?

_____

_____

_____

99.  Do you have any other financing that will be paid off with your new proceeds? _____

_____

100. If so, what and how much? _____

_____

_____

101. Do you have any cosigners or other guarantors for your new proceeds? Who?

_____

_____

_____

102. Do you have controlling interests in other businesses?  _____

103. Are there any supporting documents you can use that will help your solidify your claims to the investor/lender (newspaper articles, quotes by industry experts, magazine articles, brochures, graphs, charts, copies of contracts, etc.)?

_____

_____

_____

104. How do you produce your product or service (internally/in-house, externally/subcontract, etc.)?

_____

_____

_____

105. Will your current production philosophy change in future years? If so how?

_____

_____

_____

106. What is your current production capacity in units of output and in dollars on a monthly basis?

_____

_____

_____

107. Can your current facility handle future growth demands?

_____

_____

_____

108. Have you established lead times for the ordering of inventory?

_____

109. Does your current facility allow for flexibility with regard to growth?

_____

110. If a new building is being considered, have you planned for:
    a. Adequate warehouse/office space for future expansion? _____
    b. Efficient loading docks and ground-level door entrances? _____
    c. Ease of transportation to roadways, railroads and airports? _____
    d. Convenient to customers and suppliers? _____

111. Have you properly negotiated your lease (lease rates, free rent, term of lease, responsibility for roof repairs and maintenance, etc.)? _____

112. What are your lease rates? _____

113. Has your facility been properly designed to allow for efficient use of space and productivity in:
    a. Office? _____
    b. Warehouse? _____

114. Is your facility accessible to the handicapped? _____

# Appendix  2

# Sample Business Plan

*Kites rise highest against the wind,*
*not with it.*
—Sir Winston Churchill

**A Business plan for:**

**CC Day Care Center**

**Lili Lako**

**355 Academy Street**

**Orangetown, New Jersey 07999**

**(973) 555-4036**

**June 15, 2005**

# Contents

# Summary

*CC Day Care Center (CC)* will be formed in July 2005 in the city of South Orange, New Jersey, as a partnership. The dynamic team that will be responsible for the daily operations of the day-care center will be the manager director (Lili Lako), a personal assistant, an accounts clerk, an administrative staff member, three lead teachers, and two teachers' aides. CC will hire professional company secretaries, auditors, and maintenance personnel to handle these three aspects of the business. This business promises to be very lucrative for the following reasons:

1. There is a great need for an excellent day-care center in the city; at present there are none. The actual market for this service is substantial (the child population is 87,570), and has potential 20 percent annual growth in the next two to three years.
2. The initial target market, which is only 2 percent of the ultimate target market, has virtually no competitors, and this gives CC the easy entrance it needs at the start.
3. The prime location in the upper-class Kenny Hills area is ideal for a center of this nature, and the residents are willing to pay for the services that will be offered.
4. CC's ability to accomplish its goals and lead in the industry is significantly related to the know-how and ability of the management to recognize the great need of the area and seize the opportunity to capitalize on it. The high standards that CC will set will make it difficult for unscrupulous competitors to enter the market. This will reduce the competition to only those who can match the high quality of service set by CC and still be able to make a profit.

As a result of these conditions, CC believes that it has a unique opportunity to provide the best quality service in the city at very appealing prices and capture a sizable portion of the while market in five years.

# Company Analysis

## Background of the Company

*CC Day Care Center* will be the name of the child care service to be started in South Orange, New Jersey, in 2005. The company is named after Lili Lako's (LL) three-year-old daughter, Carol Christen.

CC Day Care Center (CC) will be a partnership. LL's husband, Stuart Lako (ST), will be the other partner, who will initially assist in setting up the business. ST is business major who has vast experience as an entrepreneur. Currently, ST is the owner of a medium-sized advertising agency in South Orange. ST wants to broaden his business base and is therefore looking to invest in other services. ST also has a wide network of business associates who are looking for lucrative businesses to invest in; this will be extremely useful in the near future should the need arise for more capital.

LL will be responsible for the daily running of the business. The main purpose of the company is to provide an all-day child care service to the upper-class community of *Kenny Hills* in South Orange. The average income in Kenny Hills is about $100,000 annually. There is currently no such child care service offered in the area.

Initially, there will be one personal assistant, at least one administrative and accounting staff member, and the other personnel will consist of lead teachers (master's in education) and teachers' aides (i.e., teaching certified but trained by CC's own lead teachers). The number of personnel will grow with the increase in the number of children per day. The ratio of teachers to children will be about 1 to 15, and this is to be the initial selling point. The wealthy are very concerned about the personal attention their kids are receiving; they do not mind paying for this attention.

## Service Offered

The philosophy of CC is based on the following:

1. Children between the ages of three and six cannot stand conformity, so their work will be less structured. However, their curriculum will include math, english, science, social studies, and an additional language taught through the latest methods (through games, cooperative learning, etc.).

2. Children should be self-directed. This concept teaches the children to work independently of the teacher. This will be preparation for the future when the company has grown. This new concept that "a

small class does not necessarily mean better" will to be introduced with utmost care because we began with just the reverse as our

3. The children here will taught to be self-motivated, to survive in any environment, and to have positive self-images. Positive reinforcement will be highlighted.

4. The service should meet high standards, which will be monitored closely; the "homey" yet professional educational support provided will be the key ingredient.

The service CC will be offering will be aimed at rich families where the parents are occupied with their own careers and need to be assured that their children are safe while being educated. Many rich wives may not have careers of their own but may have social obligations that take them away from their homes. They, too, need to be confident that their kids' needs are well taken care of!

## Market and Customers

The major market that CC will serve will be the wealthy community of the Kenny Hills region in the heart of South Orange. There are many such rich communities in the city, but this will be the first group focused on. The total population of this area is approximately 3,600; however, CC initially will be addressing only about 10 percent of this market. This is mainly due to the limited capital; CC's owners will "dig deep into their pockets" because they do not want to start the business with the heavy burden of debt.

## Capital

The capital that has been set aside for the business is between $65,000 and $75,000; this will include the initial start-up cost plus the cost of all the necessary equipment that is required of a business of this nature (see list under "Operation Resources"). The return on investment that is expected of CC is 30 percent per year.

## Customers

Although the principal customers will be those whose annual income is $100,000 and above, the *upper middle class* will be CC's peripheral customers. These people also want the best for their children and will strive to achieve this. The common denominator among these customers will be their concern for reliability and professionalism coupled with the latest teaching techniques.

## Competition and Location

The fact that the closest day-care center of any kind is ten miles away is also a point in CC's favor. The other centers are mainly for groups of people with lower incomes. There are other small, private centers, but they are all mediocre, not very reputable, and are located on the far side of town. CC will be strategically located in a building that is already being reserved; the contract is currently being drawn up by our lawyers. This building has been examined by the local authorities and is deemed fit for a child care service business.

According to a national survey, more than 57 percent of men and 85 percent of women have trouble finding child care facilities. This need for more child care facilities has been brought to the attention of state legislatures, many of which—along with the federal government—provide subsidies for low-income families in need of baby-sitting services. However, most parents realize that baby sitters cannot provide the structured learning activities necessary in early childhood development.

## Strengths

The primary strength will be its location and the fact that it will be one of the first preschools of such caliber in the city of South Orange. The child care center will be nearer the parents' homes. Studies show that parents prefer to leave their children nearer their homes than their offices, and for this reason, centers do better in or near residential areas. Also, mothers need to feel that their kids are close by should the occasion arise that the mothers need to see them.

The other fact is that there are no other competitors in this lucrative segment of the market. The preschool population (i.e., children between ages of three and six) is rising. It is up by 10.2 percent in the past few years. Current projections call for the population of children under the age of six to increase by a further 8 percent.

## Weaknesses

Because this will be a new setup, it will take some time before the center will be able to rely on word-of-mouth as its dominant marketing tool. The company will have to use the Yellow Pages and other advertising devices to make CC known. However, the establishment will be able to use both LL's and ST's networks to reach many potential customers. Because LL will be the only one providing a service of this nature in this location, achieving recognition should not pose much of a problem. As the venture takes off and the company establishes its reputation, the parents of the enrolled kids will be the company's salespeople.

## Technology and Backward Integration

The most dominant feature here will be the latest teaching methods incorporated in the school curriculum. CC will have to update its facilities and mode of instruction by regularly sending its teachers for training. The director will also have to go abroad to find new ways of tapping the young minds at CC. The use of computers in the classroom will definitely be a must.

Farther down the line, CC will be a backward-integrated company—it will control some of its supply systems (e.g., the company that supplies all the stationary and elementary supplies necessary for schools). It may even go into the nutrition business and supply all meals made available at CC.

## Operation Resource

The facility that will house the business allows for 35 square feet of space per child indoors and 50 to 70 square feet per child outdoors. Because the teachers will probably never have all the children outside at once, it is required that LL designate the play space per child for only the children who will be outdoors at any given time. (See Appendix B for "child oriented environment.") There will also be ample parking space. The minimum requirement for 30 children will be two toilets and basin for boys and the same for girls. To save on plumbing costs, the bathrooms will be located adjacent to existing adult-sized bathrooms.

Since all children will assigned a cot, they can store their personal belongings on their cots to eliminate the need for a special storage area. Below is a list of some of the equipment CC will need:

1. Classroom stacking chairs
2. Round and rectangular tables
3. Cots, pillows, cot sheets, cot blankets
4. Storage cabinets (for toys and educational materials)
5. Tape dispensers
6. Set of state-approved swings
7. Slides
8. Sandboxes
9. Set of monkey bars
10. Stove, oven, other kitchen utensils
11. Refrigerators, freezers
12. Dishwashers, electric-mixer
13. Three-compartment sink

Office equipment also will be necessary, such as a computer used a record-keeping system.

LL will provide snack and main meals if they are requested by the parents. There will be an extra charge for these meals. (See Appendix C for a guide to child care food.) Though LL will have a few suppliers to buy from, she will run checks on the food to ensure that high standards of safety, hygiene, and balanced meals are maintained. There are many savings that can be obtained by making orders in large quantities. Because CC is an all-day child care service, most parents opt for the full-meal plan as opposed to the partial-meal plan. The additional cost per child will be between $5 and $10 per child per day.

## Costs

The initial capital LL will need to start this business is $65,000, which will come from family savings. The service CC is offering will cost the customer between $400 and $500 per month. This payment will cover the cost of rental, equipment, advertising, utilities, professional services, owner salary, payroll, supplies, insurance, and other expenses. The projected gross sales will be between $144,000 and $180,000 (depending on whether the fee is $400 or $500 per child per month). The fee charged initially will be $400, and after six months (after market penetration) the fee will be increased to $500. This increase will be simultaneous with CC's new requirement for higher qualified teachers. The lead that CC will take in raising the standards of day-care centers in the region will justify the increase in the price.

The main costs that can deplete the finances will be the purchase of equipment. Therefore, LL will have to take great care in monitoring this element. To curb wastage, it is imperative that LL first decides on the teaching activities before ordering the needed tools. The other element that should be handled with care is the payroll—CC will need the best teachers and yet LL will have to watch the costs. If LL is able to keep the costs low and yet maintain high teaching standards, CC will definitely be assured of success. The self-motivated, confident, and intelligent children will be CC's best advertisers.

# Industry Analysis

## The Child care Industry Definition, Size, and Growth

The child care industry includes all child care services for children between the ages of three and six; this includes all-day care and education. For a start, CC will appealing to those parents who are earning $100,000 and more per year—the upper-class community of Kenny Hills.

The actual size of the entire child population of South Orange is 87,570. The eventual target market is about 21,892 children (2000 figures from the Bureau of the Census) who will be able to afford to attend CC DAY CARE CENTER (CC). However, the current target market will be expected to grow by at least 20 percent in the next two to three years due to the growth in the economy; this growth is also based on the assumption that people will become more affluent and that more parents will migrate to this city because of better, more lucrative job opportunities in South Orange.

Currently, CC has no competitors in this industry (that is, in the Kenny Hills location). This residential area is deal for a child care center of this nature. It is also opportune because the government will be launching a nationwide "Educational Awareness Program" shortly. Presently, there are no special (qualification) requirements for teachers in these centers. LL will begin to set some standards by ensuring that the teachers have a minimum qualification of an undergraduate degree in early childhood education. There are many well-trained teachers who are currently employed by the public sector because there are no lucrative job offers in the private sector. CC will begin the trend and allow teachers more job opportunities while raising the standards of day-care centers. Later, CC will raise the requirements further by insisting that lead teachers have a master's degree in early childhood education.

The forward trend in this industry is that day-care centers are expected to mushroom everywhere because the standards of education are rising, and parents want to give their children the competitive edge. There are no startling trends in technology, except for personal computers to maintain the database of students. The prevailing preschools, kindergartens, and day-centers are synonymous and are just play schools for the kids to pass their time in safety while their parents are busy with their own careers. Some of the better centers do offer rudimentary teaching of the alphabet, but only one offers the basics of "reading, writing, and 'rithmetic." This one is called "Marguerite" and is ten miles away from CC's location.

The statistical arm of the government reports that all the government-sponsored centers are welfare-oriented—that is, they cater to the lower income bracket.

## Cyclical Influences and Seasonality

LL believes that CC's long-term performance will not rise and fall as a result of external economic cycles. There will always be a need for a good school like CC, regardless of how good or how poor the economy is; during good times the parents can afford and want to give the best to their kids; during bad times both parents may need to work to supplement their income, but they invariably want the best for their children. Generally, this type of business should do well, especially since CC's target is the wealthy. Also, CC should do very well because it has no competitors in this locality.

The distribution of business activity throughout the year will not affect CC because the fees (inclusive of registration and all other related fees) for school are paid even if there are holidays. In fact, most parents will pay their registration fees very early to ensure their children are guaranteed a place in the respective schools. All fees fall due on the first of every month.

## Financial Operating Characteristics

Through extensive research done by LL's partner, ST, we have arrived at the respective financial (Profit & Loss Account) estimates found in Appendix F.

## The Working Paper for Setting Up CC

### Assumptions and Notes

The study is limited to the preschool population in the city only. There is no point in going beyond this because the transport problems are tremendous, not to mention other obstacles.

CC will begin by charging a flat fee of $400 per month for the first six months. This is because the teachers CC will be employing will require only a bachelor's degree in early childhood education. Currently, the law does not require these teachers to possess any special qualifications. However, later CC will upgrade its teachers, and will require lead teachers to have a master's degree in early childhood education. Hence, the fee will then be increased to $500. Also, the classes will also get bigger, and CC will change the teaching emphasis. The selling point will be the independent learning abilities of the children. The children will be taught to be self-motivated and excel in any environment—this will be the new marketing strategy.

### Sales

Purchases relate to those expenses that can be directly charged to CC's clients, that is, the students. For example, it may cost $7.50 per day to feed each child. The other costs will be called "overheads." Overhead costs are incurred in the running of the school but can only be "apportioned" to each pupil on a per-head basis. This is because the cost is usually "indirectly" incurred. The formula is Cost per Student X Number of Children X Number of Days in the Month.

### Bank Charges

A fixed figure for the charges will be assumed because of the service charges and interest rates levied by the bank on any overdrafts that CC may apply for. To be conservative, LL has provided for $200 per month.

### Director's Salary

LL will assume a director's salary of $3,000 per month.

### Entertainment and Refreshments

The budget for the monthly entertainment and refreshment expenditure will be $1,000. This refers to the expense involved in going out to meet prospective students and their parents.

### Insurance

The going rate for a general liability medical/accident policy for the children is $10 per child.
Formula: Insurance Rate x Number of Children per Month.

### Medical Fees

CC will provide some medical benefits for the staff—this covers only minor ailments. A rough estimate based on recent estimates of medical costs is $150 per month.

### Newspapers and Periodicals

CC will subscribe to daily newspapers and other relevant periodicals that enable the center to keep up with the latest developments in the industry and in the city. This will cost $200 per month.

### Postage

This is directly related to administration and is expected to increase with the number of children.

### Printing and Stationery

Documents like letterheads and invoices have to printed. Other office supplies are also included and the total cost is estimated to be $5,000, which will be paid for at the start of the business.

### Rental

This expense will form the largest single item of overhead. Sufficiently large premises must be rented to accommodate at least five hundred kids—this allows for predetermined expansion. The contract is currently being examined by our lawyers, the and cost of renting the premises is expected to be $10,000 per month.

### Salaries

Salaries are forecast to be as follows:
- personal assistant at $2,000 per month
- teacher ($900 per month initially; later at $1,800 per month)
- administrative clerk
- accounts clerk at $800 per month

### Secretarial and Accounting Fee

The company will use outside professional company secretaries and auditors to manage these two aspects respectively. The present rate for these services is $1,800 per year. It can be apportioned over the period of twelve months, thus making a monthly fee of $150.

### Telephone

Telephone charges fluctuate from month to month. As there is no precedent for estimating such charges, CC would be wise to provide a "safe" amount to cover any contingencies that may arise. $500 per month should be adequate.

### Maintenance

The center will use an outside professional maintenance company to ensure the premises are clean. The going rate is $350 per month.

*Utilities*

The utilities will increase with the enrollment. The increase is projected at 10 percent per month based on the figures provided by the city utilities department.

*Advertisement*

Advertisements will be essential at the outset. Since the reputation of the establishment will not have been established, selection of a "media mix" is essential to the center. The medium that CC will select will be TV and radio. The local newspaper (rates of the major newspaper are seen in Appendix G) and the Yellow Pages will be the other advertising media. Hence, the initial cost of $10,000.

*Leasing*

The capital expenditure for this business will be mainly on the equipment required; this will, however, be leased at the rate of 8 percent over 3 years. Thus, these payments work out to be $2,584 per month.

Break-Even at start-up is:

$$S=FC+VC$$
$$1000S=38,609,000=405S$$
$$S=\$64,889$$

Break-Even for beginning of year two is:

$$S=FC+VC$$
$$595S=52,451,000$$
$$S=\$88,153$$

Therefore, it is projected that CC will need $88,153 in sales to break even and anything more will be a profit. It can be seen that at the end of the first year CC should have $137,888 (accumulated profit/loss).

# Market Analysis

## Market/Location

Recent Studies have shown that more than 50 percent of children are in need of day care. The need is even greater among the wealthy. There is a dire need for excellent child care facilities, and this has been brought to the attention of the federal government. Home baby-sitting services have been sprouting around the city, but most parents realize that these baby sitters cannot provide the structured learning activities necessary in early childhood development. Besides, the authorities have also exposed some of these services as "scams." There also have been some cases of child abuse brought to light in connection with these home businesses, which has caused many parents to skeptical about such setups.

Consequently, a more structured and professionally run day-care center will be received very well, especially by the wealthy populace. Once of the most significant trends is the increase of women in the workforce. As such, CC will be a welcome relief to these career-conscious women. The actual size of the entire market is 87,570 (i.e., children between the ages of three and six). The company's target market is the 21,892 kids (2000 figures from the Bureau of the Census) whose parents will be able to afford to send their children to CC. However, the initial market will be just 2 percent (439 kids in the wealthy Kenny Hills area) of the ultimate target market. This market is expected to grow by at least 20 percent within the next three years for reasons mentioned in the Industry Analysis section.

Studies show that working parents prefer to leave their children nearer home than office. For this reason, CC will do better in this residential area. The rich in this neighborhood have at least one maid per household. These maids will be able to tend to the needs of the kids more readily if the children are located near their homes. The parents in this region tend to be very well educated and in one of the highest income brackets in the country. Generally, these people are young to middle-aged CEOs of huge corporations, and own homes worth more than $500,000. Many of these residents have inherited much of their wealth from affluent ancestors.

The wealthy community of Kenny Hills is situated in the heart of South Orange and is very strategically located—it is within easy reach of all the modern conveniences: communication centers, transportation, commercial and banking centers, shopping centers, etc. Its central location makes Kenny Hills easily accessible, and yet this unique, mature dwelling of the rich is very private in layout.

## Economic Base

The wealth of this community has already been determined and mentioned in the Company Analysis section. Hence, with an average family income of $100,000 per year, CC's opportunities seem very bright. The houses here are valued at a minimum of $500,000 and the percentage of ownership is 95 percent.

## Important Factors for Site Selection

### Accessibility

The parents will have easy access to CC's site when dropping their children off. The center is situated on a corner location at the end of a two-lane street; it is a private road that does not have a heavy flow of traffic since it is in a private residential area. However, it is easily accessible, because there are "feeder" roads that turn off into the main street. Therefore, congestion is reduced and, because the speed of traffic is not more than 20 miles an hour, drivers will not have difficulty entering or leaving the site.

### Rent

The working paper with the sales-and-profit projection for the first year of operations was discussed in the Industry Analysis. It was clearly shown how CC forecasted a gradual increase of sales (from $12,000 to $180,000) through the first year of operation. A market Analysis of the Forecast Monthly Sales is shown in Appendix F.

The rental is seen (in Appendix F) to be as high as 80 percent of total sales in the beginning of the business, but by the end of the first 12 months it is projected to be just 5 percent of total sales. This is because the rental is quite high in this premium rental area. It is also observed that the enrollment will begin with just 12 kids and increase to 360 (30 times the initial number) by the end of the first year. As this flat rent is for two years, it will remain as a fixed cost of $10,000 throughout the contractual period.

## Parking

CC will provide easy, adequate parking and access for its customers. Since this building used to be a finishing school for girls, it has a parking area that is relatively new and does not need resurfacing; this means no additional costs to CC.

## History of the Site

This building used to be a finishing school for wealthy girls, but the school has been relocated to smaller premises and has been changed to a holiday camp because the needs of its customers have changed.

## Advertising

At the beginning CC will have to select a good "media mix" to enhance the business as the reputation of the center has not yet been established. The medium that CC will select in which to place its commercials will be TV and radio. The local premier daily (the rates of this major newspaper are displayed in Appendix G) and the Yellow Pages will be the other advertising media.

"An effective media mix should have a synergistic effect on its components" (*Yellow Pages* and the *Media Mix*, p. 1). CC's potential customers must see a newspaper ad, hear a radio spot, and see a TV commercial to reinforce the company's message at the outset of business. The impact of these potential customers will be far greater if CC uses the "media mix" rather than just one of these media.

## Television

Television is the second largest advertising medium. It is the most dynamic of all forms of advertising because it combines visual activity and sound. Its broad appeal and large audience will definitely work for the center.

However, CC has a relatively small audience, so the company will only advertise in the immediate area. TV is relatively expensive, so the spots will be selected very carefully to capture the right audience at prime time.

### Radio

This is the most universal of all media. The average American has three radios per household and most cars are also equipped with one. The air times will be selected carefully because the target audience is very important to the organization. The cost for radio advertising is relatively low and is usually within the reach of many small businesses. The major drawback of radio advertising is the absolute need for repetition.

### Newspapers

There are six main newspapers in the area and the Survey Research Department maintains that the *New York Times* is most widely read and circulated. This is the newspaper that is read by every household in the Kenny Hills area. The cost is relatively low and there is reader loyalty. However, because the life span is very short there will be a need for repeat ads. However, CC will be able to take advantage of the discounts being offered for "run-ons" (i.e., discounts for ads running 3 days in a row). The detailed advertising rates are listed in Appendix G.

Newspapers appeal to a diverse range of age groups and income levels; however, since this is the main publication distributed in the area, it will assist CC to expand its market in later years. Newspapers, like radio, can offer advertisers the ability to target their audiences with precision (*Yellow Pages* and the *Media Mix*, p. 3, 4). The greatest advantage of this medium of advertising is flexibility; the amount of advertising is not limited, as in TV or radio, by the constraints of time. Advertisers are not limited to just one format—they can choose a full page, a two-page spread, or even buy space by the column-inch. On the other hand, newspapers have a very short life span, and like the radio, need a high degree of repetition to be effective.

### The Yellow Pages

The Yellow Pages is a fast-growing advertising medium. The advertising functions of this medium are different from the other media. It does not work by creating an awareness of or a demand for CC's services; instead, it points willing customers in the direction of where this service can be had. The Yellow Pages is a "directional" medium. CC will use this medium to attract new customers who are willing to spend their money.

CC will be highly successful in the Yellow Pages because currently, it has no competitors in its niche of the market. The users of this directory are, generally, young to middle-aged, relatively well-educated, employed professionally or as managers, living in metropolitan areas, and financially well off. The Yellow Pages is in great demand and is used both at home and at places of business.

Eventually, the most important marketing tool will be by word-of-mouth. CC will inevitably concentrate on this tool. As the company's reputation grows, CC will move away from all other modes of advertising and the advertising cost will be lowered considerably. In this line of business when one is dealing with parents (who are almost always concerned with the reliability and reputation of the school and its staff), all other marketing devices will not work. Eventually, most, if not all, of the children enrolled at CC will be as a result of positive referrals. The parents of these kids will be CC's true salespeople.

# Management Team

## Employee Qualifications

Currently, the law requires only minimum qualifications for the staff in day-care centers. However, when CC first goes into business there will be a general requirement demanded of all the personnel. The staff will be screened carefully to ensure that CC secures people to ensure that the center will be able to offer the best service in the area.

Before hiring, the two partners will write down the following: (1) a job description, including the objectives of the job, the work performed, responsibilities, working conditions, and relationships to other jobs; and (2) the job specifications, that is, a description of the qualifications required to fill the particular job, including experience, education, special skills, and any physical requirements. See Appendix A for a sample to be adapted for CC's use.

Because CC will be taking care of children, the interview of the potential employee will be conduct din a manner that will enable the interviewer to learn as much as possible about the interviewee. CC will employ only the "trouble-free" applicants.

## Duties

### The Director

As the owner/director, LL's job initially will include almost everything. The director will provide the necessary hiring, training, supervising, planning the curriculum and scheduling, budgeting, making purchases, promoting the business, setting up the books, handling enrollments, solving problems, and so on. Fortunately, the other partner, Mr. Stuart Lako, will help in this area, too. They will employ professional help in many of the above areas to ensure that the company starts off on its best foot.

There will be a personal assistant to help with running the business. This person will have a degree in education or early childhood development, and will also have good communication skills and be able to relate equally well to both parents and children. There are many retired teachers with both organizational ability and expertise in dealing with young children. These retirees are currently unable to find any useful employment. It will be relatively easy to get the cream of the crop now.

## Staff

CC will start with one college-trained teacher for every fifteen children, as mentioned in the Company Analysis. CC will set the standards for quality. To ensure that this center will be the leader in this industry, it will maintain very high standards as it becomes more established—always ahead, always getting better. The center will begin with just college-trained teachers, and later, as mentioned in the Industry Analysis, will hire graduate lead teachers and undergraduate teachers' aides.

The monthly salary was taken care of in the Industry Analysis. As the profits increase and the requirements change, so will the salaries (from

$900 to $1,800). Children are fragile people, so the people handling them will have to be loving, mature, and healthy, with positive attitudes about life, love, and interpersonal relations. It must be noted that kids are very intelligent and extremely impressionable and will pick up attitudes and behaviors of the adults around them with amazing accuracy. The aides must also be instinctively adept at disciplining children fairly without traumatizing them. Finally, they must have the skills to implement play and instructional activity for groups of disorganized, rambunctious, strong-willed youngsters.

## Other Employees

The company will hire professional company secretaries and auditors to manage these two aspects of the business. The present rate is a monthly fee of $150. There will also be an accounts clerk and an administrative staff member, who will each be paid $400 per month. The center will be maintained by professional maintenance personnel to ensure the premises are clean. The going rate is $350 per month.

Recruiting employees for this business will be limited by geography. There is no competition currently, so there will not be much competition to contend with in regards to "pinching" good staff members. However, as the company grows, CC will ensure that it shares its profits with the staff to ensure that the better members will remain with the organization. We will pay them what the market requires—with significant increase once they have proved themselves, because "two motivated, well-paid, capable employees will serve one better than three mediocre, lackadaisical, underpaid ones." Weak employees hurt the morale of the others, so they will have to go.

## Good Personnel Policies

CC will go out and recruit staff at universities and schools, at established government and private employment agencies, and through referrals from friends and other business firms. Advertising in local daily publications can also be effective, but only if advertising expense is reasonable or the position requires special training.

References will have to be checked carefully, and extended interviews will be conducted to *weed out the undesirable*. Initially, salaries will reflect market rates or better, if this can be justified. There will be an annual review of each employee's progress and productivity. These reviews will be discussed with the employees so that they will know where they stand with the company.

Fringe benefits, health and hospital insurance, profit-sharing plans, pensions, and paid vacations with all be part of a complete personnel program. All successful business owners recognize that fair wages, attractive fringe benefits, desirable working conditions, and concern for employees are important in building a dedicated, efficient staff. Such staff will advance CC's goals, and by word-of-mouth, create an image of this company as a good place to work.

## Build Employee Morale

CC will accept and use the ideas of the company's employees and give them full credit if the idea is successful. This will definitely encourage employee contributions and cooperation and create a true spirit of accomplishment. Employee morale and team spirit are important to the success of this company. Regulations with regards to salaries and minimum work hours will be strictly adhered to.

## Hidden Costs of Employment

CC figures that 12 percent above total salaries will cover payroll taxes, worker's insurance, and paid vacation. There is also a portion that has to be paid into the employee retirement fund to take care of their retirement benefits. This amount is around 8 percent at present.

The failure or degree of success will often be related to the quality of employees in the organization. CC will develop professional and psychological techniques to use in the interviews to ferret out hard, smart workers (*AEA Business Manual #X1058, Business Startup Guide*).

# Strategic Planning

## Goals of the Company

CC Day Care Center will make its debut in the Kenny Hills area as the first excellent day-care center in South Orange. As it becomes a more established organization throughout the city, it will branch out into other similar locations. After the third year of operation, CC should have an enrollment of at least 1,080 children (i.e., about three times the enrollment at the end of the first year).

After the first three years of operation, CC will be well known for its advanced teaching methods and will expand into other markets. This will be a good time to venture to capture the upper-middle and the middle class. CC will be in a better position to command a bigger share of this market.

In its fourth year of operation, CC will make its facilities available to toddlers from families who are in the lower income bracket. This will be a nonprofit organization and will be run to aid less fortunate children. This will be CC's way of making its contribution to society. This center will be run in conjunction with some of the government programs available, making use of teachers provided by the state but retrained by CC. This project will be done as a separate undertaking to help society and also to gain some goodwill for CC. The center will want to move away from the public image that CC is an organization only for the rich; this, then, will be a good time for CC to move into the bigger market—the entire northern portion of New Jersey.

## Operations

### *Admissions Policies and Procedures*
In the initial step of the interview, the parent and the child will be given a guided tour of CC's child care facility. This gives the director an opportunity to sell the advantages of structured play and instruction with other children over simple baby sitting. Simultaneously, the exposure to the equipment, play areas, and other children will excite the child.

Almost all working parents know the need for child care, so CC's sell will be a soft one, allowing the cleanliness, friendliness, and efficiency of the facility to be observed. Next, the director will determine the days and the hours that parents will need the child care services. Monday through Friday will be best because most parents prefer that their children have the weekends off. The rate schedule will be presented, along with a brochure describing the goals, curriculum, and services of this excellent center.

As part of the contract, the parents pay for the first term (the first three months) in advance, and then the child is scheduled to begin. CC will accept all children between the ages of three and six because this is common practice. The children will then be evaluated and placed in their respective classes; they will b allowed to progress at their own pace.

The children will not be placed in the conventional A, B, and C classes, as has been the prevalent practice in the past. This categorizing only makes the slower child feel bad and slows rather than advances his or her progress; it reinforces his or her slow capabilities. This labeling has proved to be detrimental to the well-being of such a child. Instead, children at CC will be evaluated according to their skills in reading, writing, arithmetic, etc., and when these classes are scheduled children will be regrouped according to their levels. The older children in the classes will seem to be teaching the younger ones. Children are always learning from each other, and they learn faster this way, too. Of course, this will all be done under the guidance of the teacher.

An enrollment card will be filled out by the parent, stating the child's name, address, names of parents or guardians and their home and office phone numbers, the days and hours of attendance, the child's medical insurer and policy number, and any special conditions regarding the child. A short statement of the limited liabilities and responsibilities of the facility will be printed on the card, read by the parent or guardian, and signed. This will be done in accordance with applicable law.

### Food Service

The children at CC will be provided with complete menus for well-balanced meals throughout the week. This will be made possible by engaging one of the many food specialist services in the city. The food costs will be budgeted carefully, keeping a tight range of costs for the feeding of each child. It will cost about $5 per day per child: this will include breakfast, lunch, and a light snack. The light snack will be around 3 p.m. because most parents prefer to have dinner with their children between 7:30 p.m. and 8:30 p.m.

### Suggested Daily Program

Schedules will be set up with the help of the directors and in accordance with the relative curriculum. See Appendix E for the guide from which CC will adapt its curriculum. The following schedule shows the kinds of activities that will be organized for the facility:

| | |
|---|---|
| 7:00 a.m. to 8:00 a.m. | Arrivals |
| 8:00 to 8:30 | Breakfast |
| 8:30 to 9:00 | Show-and-Tell Time |
| 9:00 to 9:30 | Individual Projects |
| 9:30 to 10:00 | Cooperative Learning |
| 10:00 to 10:30 | Snack time |
| 10:30 to 11:00 | Free Play |
| 11:00 to 11:30 | Learning Skills |
| 11:30 to 12:00 noon | Fun with Math |
| 12:00 noon to 1:00 p.m. | Group Singing |
| 1:00 p.m. to 2:30 | Rest Time |
| 2:30 to 3:00 | Snack Time |
| 3:00 to 4:00 | Learning Skills |
| 4:00 to 5:00 | Story Time and pickup at school |

The above schedule serves only as a guide; good child care programs are not as regimented; indeed, they are flexible enough to vary with the day-to-day temperaments of the children. The key here is flexibility—that is essential when handling children.

### Transportation

Delivery and pickup of these children will inevitably be done by their parents or their chauffeurs, as they all come from wealthy households. Therefore, there will not be any extra costs incurred by CC to purchase vans or small school buses to transport the children to and from home.

### Medical Problems

If an accident should occur while the child is at the center and immediate treatment is needed, the child will be taken to the emergency room of the nearest hospital, with his medical insurance information and parents' names and numbers. The hospital will inform the parents and obtain a verbal medical release.

All staff members will be required to have first-aid training, with at least one person CPR certified. A small isolation room for the sick will be made available on the premises. The teachers will be required to give their respective students a quick checkover each morning. Any potentially contagious disease is a danger to the health of other children and employees, hence, care will have to be exercised in this area.

### Regulations

CC will meet all regulations affecting the child care industry. CC will be the leader in this industry and maintain very high standards in the operation of the facility.

### Monthly Operating Statement

This is examined in great detail in the Industry Analysis (also refer to Appendix F). It is clear that the average monthly revenue will be $92,250 and the average money expenses will be $42,401, therefore making the new profit before tax $48,848. The gross profit will be $54,892. The net profit as a percentage of gross sales in the first year will be 52.95 percent.

### Failure Factors

CC will take special care to avoid making the same mistakes that other entrepreneurs have made in the past. Constant market research or seeking help form a consultant will help resolve some of the major problems.

Most small business surveys show that the primary reasons for failure lie in the following areas:

1. Inefficient control over costs and quality of service

2. Bad stock control

3. Underpricing of service

4. Bad customer relations

5. Failure to promote and maintain a favorable public image

6. Bad relations with suppliers

7. Inability to manage efficiently

8. Failure to keep pace with management system

9. Illness of key personnel

10. Reluctance to seek professional assistance

11. Failure to minimize taxation through tax planning

12. Inadequate insurance

13. Loss of impetus in sales

14. Bad personnel relations

15. Loss of key personnel

16. Lack of staff training

17. Lack of knowledge of the service

18. Inability to cope adequately with competition.

19. Competition disregarded due to complacency

20. Failure to anticipate relevant market trends

21. Loose control of liquid assets

22. Insufficient working capital

23. Growth without adequate capitalization

24. Bad budgeting

25. Inadequate financial records

26. Extending too much credit

27. Bad credit control

28. Bad control over receivables

29. Overborrowing or using too much credit

30. Loss of control through creditor's demands

## Market Opportunities to Exploit

The upper class in Kenny Hills is the market segment that CC will serve as described in the Company Analysis, and the Market Analysis sections. Later, in the third year of operation, the company will venture to other geographic areas to widen its market. Here the center will serve different types of customers who will offer new opportunities. As mentioned earlier, these will be middle-class households.

## Business Strategies

### Market Strategies

The strategies that CC will create initially will be the small student-to-teacher ratio to satisfy the needs of its customers. However, later on, as mentioned in the earlier section, the center will move away from this strategy and focus on the teaching techniques and technology available at the center. The high standards and highly qualified teaching staff will also be another marketing strategy used (see Appendix H).

The "media mix," as mentioned in the Market Analysis, will also be a part of the marketing strategy that CC will use to make the company a success. Television, radio, newspapers, and the Yellow Pages will be effectively used to capture the right audience and will be CC's advantage. The most effective marketing tool, word-of-mouth, will only be used when the company has established itself in the industry. At that stage in time, all the other marketing strategies will not be as effective because most of the enrollment will then be a direct result of positive referrals. The only exception will be new residents of the city.

# Financial Analysis

## Licenses and Taxes

### Licenses

The city requires that the owners of CC obtain a license to show compliance with local regulations. The owners will need to pay a fee to operate the business in the city. There is no additional fee to be paid. Obtaining the license is a simple process, as there are few laws that restrict or hinder the application procedure. CC has had the premises checked by the local authorities for safety and all of the company documentation has already been taken care of by CC's lawyers.

### Health-Department Permit

Since CC will not be preparing any food, it will not be necessary to obtain a health-department permit. The company will be purchasing its food supplies from a reputable food specialist (as mentioned in the Company Analysis).

### Fire-Department Permit

The city's fire department requires the business to have its premises inspected for safety features. However, it does not require businesses to secure a permit. CC has already been given a clean bill of health by the fire department and will be ready to begin operations as planned.

### Company Taxes

CC will have to pay a 45 percent tax on the profits. The company will be required to estimate its tax liability each year and pay it in installments if it so chooses.

At the end of each year, the organization will be required to file an income tax return for the federal and state governments and compute the tax liability on the profits earned for the year. The tax liability of the business will be calculated on a calendar year basis, and the tax return of CC must be filed with the respective department no later than April 15 of each year.

## Startup

The startup expenses and the operating capital of CC were discussed in the Company and Industry Analysis sections.

## The Business Plan

The process of creating this business plan has forced the directors of the company to take a realistic, objective, unemotional, more-or-less detached look at the proposed business in its entirety. This finished business plan will become an operating tool that will help the owners to manage and work toward its success. If financing will ever be needed, this plan will become the basis for CC's loan proposal.

## Financial Documentation

CC's key financial document is the profit-and-loss projection for the first five years (refer to Appendix F). This is the financial summary of projected income and expenses. It is clear that with the numerous initial expenses, CC will have to take losses in the first six months of operation. However, because businesses are allowed to accumulate their losses and carry forward for the first three years of operation, it is only in the month of April 1994 that profits are noted. This document shows the profit and loss at the end of each period, but it also shows the amount of money that will be on hand to operate the business. Appendix F also shows all the total expense as a percentage of the total sales.

## Financing

CC will need some financing in the third year of operation, when it plans to expand its market share. The company will get investors from among the directors' acquaintances to be able to arrange a better deal. CC's directors will assess the proposed value of the business in order to determine how much capital will be needed over specific periods of time.

The best source will be the directors themselves, of course. This is the easiest and quickest form of capital, and there is no interest to be paid. (This personal equity is reflected in the Balance Sheet in the amount $65,000.) In addition, the company will not have to surrender any equity in the child care center to "outsiders." The profits will also be carefully reinvested in the business.

The next best choice will be friends and relative of the owners. However, any money raised through this avenue will be treated as a loan. In fact, CC's lawyers will be required to draw up loan papers for each of the contributors. This legality is sought because it will prevent lenders from gaining equity in the business (unless the directors default on the loan) and it will also protect the investor's loan.

## Borrowing from Banks

The most visible sources of ready financing are banks; however, they are notoriously conservative. CC will try at all costs to avoid this avenue for various reasons.

## Selling Equity

Dividing the ownership of CC among investors is not in the plan of the organization. It is just part of a contingency plan. Selling Equity would mean that the owners would have to give up some control as well as a portion of the business. The profits would have to be shared with the new partners, depending on the setup of the establishment. The skills of good negotiators would be necessary and the services of a lawyer would be highly essential to the overall "health" of a company. It is usual for the owners to retain a 50 percent equity in the company. While the 50-50 rule is fairly common, everything is negotiable in a deal of this nature.

# Appendixes

**Author's Note:**

*List all supporting documentation in the appendix section as noted and referenced throughout your business plan. Remember, this information should be clearly and neatly presented so the reader of your business plan can easily reference and understand the data provided.*

# Appendix 3

# Sample Business Plan

*The best thing we can do is size up the chances,*
*calculate the risks involved, estimate our ability to deal*
*with them, and then make our plans with confidence.*
—Henry Ford

**A Business Plan For:**

**Micro Service and Sales**

**April 1, 2005**

**500 North Mulberry Avenue**

**Irvine, California 91455**

**(714) 555-7654**

**Rob Bradford, Owner**

# Contents

## Statement of Purpose

Micro Service and Sales, a computer sales and service firm, is a successful business that seeks financial aid to expand and continue building its profitable clientele base. The expansion would include a new location, additional inventory, and additional advertising.

The owner, Rob Bradford, desires to sell a portion of his interest in the business for the sum of $50,000. This figure includes all the money that the principle has put into Micro Service and Sales for the service equipment, spare parts, office furniture, service contracts, customer list, dealerships, and reputation.

Mr. Bradford, as well as Mrs. Bradford, would be willing to continue working for the business, building its clientele base and its reputation. Mr. Bradford seeks a salary of $2,500 per month to oversee the service and sales departments as well as the overall operation of the business. Mrs. Bradford seeks $1,000 per month to continue to do the bookkeeping, billing, and overseeing the advertising and marketing of the business on a part-time basis.

Micro Service and Sales is a successful business that needs a new location and more inventory in order to grow as it is capable of growing. The principle has put much time and effort into building the business and maintaining the highest possible reputation for honesty and hard work. An initial investment, in addition to buying out the equity of Mr. Bradford, of $56,500 for startup costs in a new location would put Micro Service and Sales on the road to becoming "the" computer store in Orange County for sales and service.

## Description of the Business

Micro Service and Sales officially began operations January 1, 2001, at 500 North Mulberry Ave. It is a sole proprietorship, owned by Rob Bradford. It is a computer sales and service operation that is open Monday through Friday, 9:00 a.m. to 5:00 p.m. However, with a relocation, Micro Service and Sales (called MSS hereafter) would be open for business Monday through Friday 10:00 a.m. to 7:00 p.m. and Saturday from 10:00 a.m. to 5:00 p.m.

MSS is a retail business that also specializes in providing the best computer repair for the best price. Along with computer repair, MSS also provides programming, consulting, and systems analysis services.

At present, the location of the business and lack of advertising funds is its only drawback. The environment is not conducive to sales and does not accommodate large numbers of people. When the business was first put into operation, the location was adequate because MSS was originally devoted to computer repair only. However, as business increased, MSS became more and more involved in sales, programming, and consulting. MSS has also become involved in more and more service and presently has service contracts with Irvine School District and California Technical College Drafting Department. MSS has grown into a successful and thriving business, and to continue its growth it must relocate.

A large part of the business comes from repeat customers for sales and service, which include Bill's Lock and Safe, Patzi's of California, Lopger Paint and Glass, PLM Systems, WK Imaging, Sunstate Equipment, Harding and Associates, GTE Phone Directories, Irvine School District, California Regional Adolescent Center, and the Orange County School District, to name just a few. California Credit Service Corporation has also been a customer for the past year and has served as a sales outlet for MSS since this time.

MSS continues to build its customer list every day, and to date MSS has customers in Arizona, New Mexico, Colorado, Texas, Oregon, Washington, and California.

The reason why MSS has been so profitable (in its first full year of operation it grossed $226,735 in sales) is the dedication and hard work of its owner. The philosophy of MSS has been and continues to be that the customer deserves the very best service, whether it is in repairing computers, selling computers, or providing customer support after the sale. Repeat business is what keeps all businesses operational, and MSS has capitalized on its ability to bring back repeat customers because the customers have received such good service. With the expansion, MSS will better serve even more of the public.

May 1, 2005, is the date by which MSS would like to be relocated and open for business. With a new location, more inventory, and a sales staff,

MSS will be one of the fastest-growing businesses in Orange County. MSS will capture a large percentage of the market share for computer sales and service because it is well organized, efficiently run, and has state-of-the-art hardware and software.

The location chosen for relocation is slated to be the best location yet in Orange County, and it offers customer-oriented service. MSS wants to be a place where people can come in for free advice and where they can feel comfortable about asking questions. MSS wants to be the place where people come to learn what is going on in the computer industry with regard to both hardware and software.

In the past, Mr. Bradford has spent a great deal of time on the phone answering questions and giving advice. He does not receive monetary compensation for this type of service, but he is paving the way for future business. When those he has helped decide to buy a computer, or have problems with one they already own, they will remember the willingness to help and positive attitude Mr. Bradford displayed.

We believe that a good majority of these people will come to MSS because of the free advice given and time spent with them by Mr. Bradford. Hopefully they will also send in their friends. Word of mouth, is by far the very best way to advertise, and that is something that cannot be forced. A business must earn trust and respect and that is what MSS will continue to do.

The previously mentioned investment capital of $55,000 will help MSS relocate to an ideal location that will produce foot traffic and generate more sales. The money will also help to buy inventory and set up MSS as a strong competitor with stores such as I-CON Computer Mart, Computers USA, and Computers of America. MSS plans to set up inventory in a showroom and make it accessible for people to use.

Many times people have in mind certain software that will only run on certain machines, and they want to see for themselves where they are making a good purchase. At present, MSS allows anyone interested in purchasing a machine to try any software they have to see if it will run. This policy has allowed MSS to sell quite a few more systems than it would have without this practice.

MSS wants to make all the systems it sells available to the public for a test drive. A computer is a major purchase, and people want to make sure they are getting the exact model they need. With the ability to try out the systems and the helpful atmosphere created by the employees, MSS will be a unique computer outlet and will be highly successful.

When a customer decides which system he or she wants and what peripherals he or she wishes to purchase, and employee will take the order. At the time the order is taken, the customer is required to pay 50 percent of the purchase price as a down payment. This deposit is nonrefundable in most cases. It is the responsibility of the employees at MSS to explain fully what the customer is paying before he or she makes a purchase.

MSS will take orders because this practice will allow MSS to keep costs down; the customer will not have to "pay" for the cost of keeping the extra inventory, which would be reflected in the price of each system. Also, ordering allows customers to get exactly what they want with all the specific options they desire. At present, MSS is able to fill orders within one week from order date and plans to continue offering this time frame. Payment in full is required on delivery. The current policy of MSS is to extend no credit, thus keeping costs down.

## Customer/Local Market Analysis

The market that MSS targets for sales is men and women 25 to 45 years old, with an annual income of $35,000 or more per year. MSS also targets the local student population at University of California at Irvine and California Technical College because more and more students are being required to use computers for their classes.

California Credit Service Corporation (CCSC) is MSS's link to the student population at the present time because CCSC lends money to students who wish to purchase a computer. Basically, the markets for MSS consist of (1) men and women who are able to purchase computer systems on their own and (2) students who borrow the money to buy the systems. These are two distinct markets that are reached through two different ways. To reach the students, MSS relies mainly on CCSC but occasionally advertises in the *Daily University Chronicle*. To reach the general public, MSS advertises in the Yellow Pages, on the radio, and through direct mailers.

Both of the markets continue to grow. National Decision Systems has estimated that the general population within a six-mile radius of the proposed relocation of MSS will increase 74,551 by 2006. The number of households within the same radius is estimated to increase 34,924 by the same time period. Currently, the student population at UC Irvine is approximately 28,264. New students make up 23 percent, integrating with the market. An additional 4 percent represents new students enrolled during the winter semester, according to UC Irvine.

The student market as well as the general public market is continuing to grow every year, and combined with the increase in computer sales, the possible market share to be captured also grows. With relocation, MSS plans to capture a larger market share by being the best-priced and most service-oriented computer store.

Concentrating on service, whether actually repairing a computer or selling a system, MSS will have a unique selling advantage. The market will accept MSS, as it already has, because of the friendly service available and the comfortable atmosphere for learning it will offer in its new location. To some people, computers seem unfriendly or hard to use, and MSS wants to bridge the gap between the public and the computers with a helpful learning environment.

MSS wants any person of any age to be able to come in and learn all they need to know about any computer and how to operate any system effectively. This policy will bring in the customers, and MSS will capture the largest market share of potential computer buyers and present computer owners and users.

MSS will also be price-conscious because Orange County tends to be very price-oriented. People want to feel that they are getting a good deal, and most people in Irvine shop around and compare prices. For this reason, MSS will also be competitively priced with the other computer stores in the area and will generally be $15 to $35 lower in price. The computer stores in the area mark up their products between 25 and 35 percent. MSS plans to mark up its products by only 25 percent. This way, MSS will be competitively priced, thus promoting the fact that MSS's products are of comparable quality and, at the same time, have some of the lowest prices available in the valley.

MSS has, in the past, discounted for package buys. For example, a customer who buys a compatible system, a printer, a modem, and a hard drive will pay less for the whole package than a customer who buys these goods at different times. MSS plans to continue this practice because it moves more inventory and makes more money for the business.

The market that MSS targets for service is mainly businesses and schools. The businesses targeted include accountants, lawyers, engineers, travel agencies, medical clinics, computer-aided design firms, and computer software firms. To reach these businesses, MSS sends out direct mailers. To reach the various schools in the area, MSS sends out letters to each principal. At present, MSS already handles the service contract for the Irvine School District and has done quite a bit of work for schools in the Costa Mesa School District.

With the markets that MSS targets for both sales and service, there is a potential to make a large amount of money. The potential of MSS, with the appropriate funds, is excellent. The principal, as well as other respected industry colleagues, believes MSS will rival any computer operation already in Orange County and any potential competition.

A greater market could be reached and maintained for sales and service with a new, more visible, more easily accessible location. Walk-in traffic, as well as advertisement response, needs a showroom area to promote sales and to "test drive" computer equipment and software. A new location would also give Micro Service and Sales the professional, competent image it seeks for growth.

## Competition Analysis

In analyzing the four main competitors, one can see that MSS will definitely have an advantage over the competition, because it will be set apart from all of the above-mentioned businesses. It is not uncommon to walk into the local retail stores and find the salespeople talking to each other and more interested in each other than in the customers. Generally speaking, the employees also lack the knowledge to really help customers. Although some of the computer stores are priced right and the employees are helpful, they lack adequate knowledge to answer technical questions.

MSS has the right prices, the right atmosphere, and the right personnel to answer questions about hardware or software. MSS has the best combination and has learned from its competitors what is desirable and what is undesirable. The only thing that any of the competition has over MSS is location. MSS has everything these stores have and more, but its location is not easily accessible, nor is it highly visible, as are the locations of our competitors.

MSS will also carry a full line of the most popular products and not devote itself to merely one type, such as IBM. MSS will be a store where anyone can find the product they need.

## Location Analysis

To bring in more revenue and build even more business, MSS should be relocated in the PlumTree Shopping Center. PlumTree is a new shopping center located at 1984 West University Drive in Irvine, California. Its target date for opening is May 1, 2005. PlumTree will have two anchor stores in the mall, one being Food-4-Less and the other being Shopko. Additional tenants are a video store, beauty shop, bakery, restaurant, and a 6-plex Cinema Theater. Extensive research has gone into this project, and the developers of PlumTree optimistically plan to make this shopping center "the hub of activity."

According to the 2003 Department of Transportation Report, 49,975 vehicles travel University Drive every day, and an additional 14,185 vehicles travel 1984 West and 7550 South. Therefore, an average of 64,160 vehicles pass by the location of this shopping center every day. University Drive is probably one of the most heavily traveled streets in all of Irvine, and PlumTree is a highly visible to this heavy traffic.

According to National Decision Systems' 2000 Census, the population has increased since 1980 is as follows:

|                  | 2-mile radius | 3-mile radius | 5-mile radius |
|------------------|---------------|---------------|---------------|
| 2005 projection  | 370,187       | 310,792       | 353,599       |
| 2000 Census      | 365,345       | 302,810       | 339,861       |
| 1990 Census      | 160,406       | 194,648       | 225,870       |
| 1980 Census      | 144,153       | 167,386       | 130,822       |

Over the past six years, median household income has increased 30 percent. According to National Decision Systems' 1990 Census, the figures are:

### Median Household Income

|               | 2-mile radius | 3-mile radius | 5-mile radius |
|---------------|---------------|---------------|---------------|
| 2005 estimate | $42,473       | $42,887       | $43,441       |
| 2000 Census   | 37,571        | 37,779        | 38,106        |

PlumTree is designed to be an easily accessible shopping center, and MSS wants to be a part of it. A move to PlumTree could realistically double, if not triple, the business that MSS already handles because of increased customer flow. The anchor store, Food-4-Less, has already signed a sixty-year lease and is expected to bring in 5500 cars per day, according to studies done in other areas where Food-4-Less is located. According to the placement of MSS in relation to the position of Food-4-Less, most of the traffic will have to pass by MSS. MSS can also be seen by those traveling University Drive.

By virtue of the fact that the shopping center is new, many people will come to see what it offers and MSS can capitalize on this. There will also be a huge grand opening for the mall and MSS will benefit from the advertisements and publicity of the newest and best location in the valley. This location will be ideal for MSS because the mall will have a grocery store, a restaurant, a video store, a bakery, and beauty salon. These businesses will draw customer traffic from which MSS will benefit. Once people know where MSS is located and have experienced the friendly, helpful attitude of its employees and compared the prices, MSS will have a substantial clientele and customer base.

The actual physical location will be on ground level with glass as its face. It will have 2,700 square feet and will have heat, electricity, and air-conditioning, as well as a bathroom for employees. The carpet and walls will reflect relaxing and nonthreatening colors. Background music will also be relaxing, promoting the comfortable feeling MSS seeks for its atmosphere. The office furniture will all be new and state-of-the-art. There will also be plants in decorative pots and decorative pictures on the walls to make people feel welcome. Smoking will not be allowed.

There is ample parking at PlumTree and accessibility to MSS will be very easy. Parking stalls will afford approximate and convenient access to the store. (Please see Appendix D for the actual layout of MSS and its position in relation to Food-for-Less.)

The location will be acquired by lease. The lease can be for one year or up to sixty years. The price is $11.50 per square foot per year. The developers estimate an additional $2.30 per square foot per year will include the utilities, landscaping and maintenance of the parking lot, fire insurance, parking-lot lighting, and garbage removal.

The increased cost of this location will be reflected in a minor price increase. However, even with the price increase, MSS plans to be as low if not lower on most items that any of its competitors. (Please see price comparisons under Competition Analysis.)

The location is yet to be completed, so the developers will work with the intended occupants to make adjustments as needed. Partition walls are needed for office and service areas and will be provided by the developers. The service area will be for repairing computers and the office will be for the secretary to do the paperwork. The developers have a set budget on what they will spend on improvements, and additional improvements must be paid for by the occupant. MSS only needs the partitions put up, so there should not be too great a cost involved in the improvements.

## Management Expertise

Rob Bradford, the owner, has been acting as chief technician, salesman, and office manager for MSS since it opened in 2001. Mr. Bradford has been involved with the computer industry since 1988. He has attended the University of California at Irvine where he studied electronic technology and also attended San Jose College where he again studied electronic technology. In 1992, Mr. Bradford went to work for IBM as a field technician. During the summer of 1994, Mr. Bradford was approached by senior management of IBM to become the director of field operations for the Southern California Region. Mr. Bradford continued as the director of field operations for IBM until he started MSS.

Mr. Bradford's expertise is mainly in IBM, IBM-compatible, and Apple computers, as well as printer and terminal repair, although his is not limited to these by any means. Aside from computers, Mr. Bradford has repaired VCRs, video cameras, televisions, and stereos. He is a capable and competent technician and manager. He has successfully managed two different businesses, the most recent being MSS.

## Support Personnel

Mrs. Bradford has served many functions at MSS. She has kept all of the books, handled the advertising and marketing, and taken care of the accounts receivable and accounts payable. She graduated from Stanford University in 1996 with a degree in advertising and sales. She has worked for various organizations including a boys' club, a theater, and Stanford University. She had no previous experience in bookkeeping but has become quite adept in maintaining orderly books. Her area of expertise is advertising, but a limited budget has not allowed her to use her talents as she would have liked. However, with an appropriate advertising budget she could increase business dramatically for MSS.

## Appropriation of Funds for Relocation and Expansion

### Initial Investment

| | |
|---|---:|
| Computer Equipment | $18,390 |
| Advertising | 7,350 |
| Furniture | 3,100 |
| Signs | 2,000 |
| Accessories for sale | 500 |
| Paperwork | 100 |
| First month's rent (includes utilities) | 2,000 |
| Three month's wages | 10,500 |
| Operating capital | 8,000 |
| Phone startup cost | 575 |
| Three-month shipping cost | 3,000 |
| First-month business insurance | 200 |

| | |
|---|---|
| First-month van insurance and gas | 285 |
| Miscellaneous (checking account) | 500 |
| **Initial Total Cost** | **$56,500** |
| Monthly Costs | |
| Rent (includes utilities) | $2,000 |
| Wages | 5,000 |
| Advertising | 1,000 |
| Phone (local, long distance, Yellow Pages ad) | 415 |
| Shipping | 1,000 |
| Business insurance | 200 |
| Paperwork | 50 |
| Van insurance and gas | 285 |
| **Total Monthly Cost** | **$9,950** |

## Summary

Micro Service and Sales is a successful, thriving business that is suffering at the moment from its location. It has a good reputation for being honest and fair. MSS has strong customer backing, but to grow as it potentially could, it needs a new location. The reason PlumTree has been chosen as its first priority for its new location is because PlumTree is a new shopping center; it is going to open with a bang, and MSS wants to be a part of it.

The developers of PlumTree feel that this shopping center is going to be better than the Mall at Orange, and they expect more than 5,500 cars per day to come through the center. MSS needs this kind of exposure. People who have brought their computers to MSS to be serviced and those who have bought their computer systems from MSS have been very pleased with the service they have received. Growth would be achieved by exposing more of the public to this kind of desirable service. Location in PlumTree shopping center would allow MSS to grow to its full potential and would pave the way for opening subsequent stores in other areas of the country.

## Partial Customer List

California Technical College
California Credit Service Corporation
Irvine Lock and Safe
Patzi's of California
Lopger Paint and Glass
LanFix
PLM Systems
WK Imaging
Strate Western
McClean Clinic
Sunstate Industries
Planned Management
Rollins, Brown and Gunnell, Inc.
Robyn Reed, International
Harding and Associates
University of California at Irvine Personnel Department
Cubco
GTE Phone Directories
Irvine School District
Regional Adolescent Center
Travel Station
Ford Construction
Riverside School District
Peripheral Equipment
Telum, Inc.
Thornhill Corp.
Frameworks
Multipoint

This list includes businesses and schools only; individuals have not been included. (Please see Appendix B for letters of recommendation.)

# Job Descriptions

## On the Payroll

*Service Manager.* The service manager oversees the operation of the service department, making sure all the repairs are done on a timely basis and that the cost of repairs is kept down for the customer. The service manager also functions as the chief technician, repairing the machines as well as overseeing the operation of the department. This is a full-time position.

*Technician.* The technician handles the service work and the service calls that the chief technician is unable to attend to. The technician also handles customer support where necessary. This can be a full-time or part-time position.

*Secretary.* The secretary takes care of all the bookkeeping, billing, bank deposits, and keeping the office inventory of staples, postage stamps, etc., up to date. This is a part-time position.

## Independent Contractors

*Advertising Director.* The advertising director makes the media buys as well as implements an advertising campaign. The advertising director is also responsible for the marketing of MSS. This position has been combined with the position of secretary in the past. This is a part-time position, and if a separate advertising director is hired, payment would be by the job.

*Sales Manager.* The sales manager oversees the sales department, making sure customers are treated well and that sales prices are competitive. This is a full-time position.

*Salespeople.* The salespeople sell the computer systems and software. These are part-time positions.

To begin, MSS would need a service manager, who would also act as chief technician; a secretary, who would also act as the advertising director; and a salesperson, who may be promoted to sales manager at a future date. The service manager and secretary would be paid salaries, while the salesperson would work strictly for commission. Additional salespeople hired in the future would also work strictly for commission. The reason the salespeople are not paid salaries is because commission-based pay tends to make people work harder and more efficiently, and top salespeople can make money for MSS as well as making a nice sum for themselves.

### Salaries

| | |
|---|---|
| Service manager | $2,500 per month |
| Secretary/advertising director | $1,000 per month |
| Future technician | $700 per month |

### Commissions

| | |
|---|---|
| Sales manager | 12 percent retail |
| Salespeople | 10 percent retail |
| Advertising director | By the job |

## Memberships

MSS is a member of the United States Chamber of Commerce, the Better Business Bureau, the National Federation of Independent Businesses, and the Orange County Chamber of Commerce. These memberships allow MSS certain privileges and also give customers confidence that MSS is a dependable and reputable business.

## Future Plans for Micro Service and Sales

In the future, MSS would like to add four to six computer systems to its inventory for instructional use and for renting to students or the general public. A rental fee of $20 per hour for the computer is a competitive price with UC Irvine; although it is not much, it would bring in additional potential customers. These units may also be used for instructional purposes, and classes could be held nightly, weekly, or monthly to teach anyone who is interested how to use a computer. An additional use for these units would be to let people come in and try out software they have already purchased or may purchase in the future. MSS would be a learning environment as much as anything else, and the customer would be the center of attention and importance.

Future plans would also include opening additional locations throughout the country. A possible second location in Orange County would be in Costa Mesa. In California, other possible locations would be San Bernardino, Riverside, Santa Barbara, San Diego, and San Francisco. A possible location in Arizona would be Phoenix. Eventually, MSS would like to be located in all of the Western states. The first chain location could be opened within two years of the relocation of MSS.

## Profit and Loss Sheet for 2004

| | | |
|---|---|---|
| January | Loss | $2,673.11 |
| February | Profit | 710.63 |
| March | Loss | 3,282.30 |
| April | Profit | 1,842.30 |
| May | Profit | 2,721.34 |
| June | Profit | 2,069.71 |
| July | Profit | 3,351.57 |
| August | Profit | 2,988.40 |
| September | Profit | 4,324.12 |
| November | Profit | 5322.08 |
| December | Profit | 9,446.62 |
| Total profit for 2004 | | $26,821.36 |

## Sales Forecast for Remainder of 2005*

New Location

| month | gross sales | gross cost | gross profit | fixed costs | net profit |
|---|---|---|---|---|---|
| May | $60,000 | $43,000 | $17,000 | $10,200 | $6,800 |
| June | 60,000 | 43,000 | 17,000 | 10,200 | 6,800 |
| July | 50,000 | 35,000 | 15,000 | 10,200 | 4,800 |
| August | 50,000 | 35,000 | 15,000 | 10,200 | 4,800 |
| September | 61,000 | 43,825 | 17,175 | 10,200 | 6,975 |
| October | 61,000 | 43,825 | 17,175 | 10,200 | 6,975 |
| November | 62,000 | 44,650 | 17,350 | 10,200 | 7,150 |
| December | 72,000 | 51,650 | 20,350 | 10,200 | 10,150 |
| Total | $476,000 | $339,950 | $136,050 | $81,600 | $54,450 |

*Figures have been rounded to nearest whole number.

To arrive at the figures above, the gross sales achieved at MSS's present location were doubled, giving the base figure of $60,000. The markup used for these calculations was 25 percent. The commission of the salesperson has also been figured into these estimates. The net profit forecasted for the remainder of 2005 at the new location is $54,450.

## Sales Forecast for 2006*

New Location

| quarter | gross sales | gross cost | gross profit | fixed costs | net profit |
|---|---|---|---|---|---|
| First | $202,025 | $146,170 | $55,855 | $40,800 | $15,055 |
| Second | 202,025 | 146,170 | 55,855 | 40,800 | 15,055 |
| Third | 202,025 | 146,170 | 55,855 | 40,800 | 15,055 |
| Fourth | 202,025 | 146,170 | 55,855 | 40,800 | 15,055 |
| Total | $808,100 | $584,680 | $223,420 | $163,200 | $60,220 |

These numbers reflect a 41 percent increase in sales from 2005, which is the estimated increase of sales according to DataFuture (November 10, 2004). The salesperson's commission has been figured into these estimates. The net profit forecasted for 2006 is $60,220.

## Sales Forecast for 2007*

New Location

| quarter | gross sales | gross cost | gross profit | fixed costs | net profit |
|---|---|---|---|---|---|
| First | $292,401 | $210,528 | $81,472 | $48,500 | $32,972 |
| Second | 292,401 | 210,528 | 81,472 | 48,500 | 32,972 |
| Third | 292,401 | 210,528 | 81,472 | 48,500 | 32,972 |
| Fourth | 292,401 | 210,528 | 81,472 | 48,500 | 32,972 |
| Total | $1,169,604 | $842,112 | $325,888 | $194,000 | $131,888 |

These figures reflect a 30 percent increase in sales from 2006, which is the estimated growth in sales according to DataFuture. The salesperson's commission has been figured into these estimates. The net profit forecasted for 2007 is $131,888.

*Figures have been rounded to nearest whole number.

# Return on Investment

New Location

| year | net profit |
|---|---|
| 2005 | $54,450 |
| 2006 | 60,220 |
| 2007 | 131,888 |
| Total net profit at end of 2007 | $246,558 |

| | |
|---|---|
| Initial investment (equity buyout of Rob Bradford) | $50,000 |
| New equipment and relocation costs | $56,500 |
| Total | $106,500 |

Net profit minus initial investment: $246,558–$106,500=$140,058

The actual net profit for the investor at the end of 2007 is $140,058 which is 131.5 percent return on the initial investment of $106,500.

# Tentative Advertising Plan, June 2005–April 2006

June

*Daily Universe*, 3 days/week, 2 x 3, 4 weeks, $351.36
*Daily Herald*, 7 days, 2 x 3, $388.08
HP Printer giveaway, $190.00

July

*Daily Universe*, 3 days/week, 2 x 3, 4 weeks, $351.36
Software giveaway, $180.00
Coupons/mailers

August

*Daily Universe*, 3 days/week, 2 x 3, 4 weeks, $351.36
*Daily Herald*, 7 days, 2 x 3, $388.08
Software giveaway, $80.00

September
    *Daily Universe*, 5 days/week, 2 x 4, 4 weeks, $958.40
    PC Paint/Mouse giveaway, $130.00
    Coupons/mailers
October
    Radio
    Modem giveaway, $95.00
November
    *Daily Herald*, 7 days, $388.08
    Software giveaway, $80.00
    Coupons/mailers
December
    Coupons/mailers
    Software giveaway, $30.00
    *Daily Universe*, 3 days/week, 2 x 3, 4 weeks, $458.64
January
    *Daily Universe*, 5 days/week, 2 x 4, 4 weeks, $958.40
    Modem giveaway, $95.00
    *Daily Herald*, 7 days, $388.08
February
    Radio
    Modem giveaway, $95.00
March
    *Daily Universe*, 3 days/week, 2 x 3, 4 weeks, $458.64
    *Daily Herald*, 7 days, $388.08
    DVD holder giveaway, $20.00
April
    *Daily Universe*, 3 days/week, 2 x 3, 4 weeks, $458.64
    Coupons/mailers
    DVD giveaway, $20.00

This is merely a tentative plan for advertising. It is dependent on how these particular media perform and whether or not they bring in customers. The budget for all months except September and January is $1,000. The budget for September and January is $1,500 to reflect additional advertising to the returning students at UC Irvine. All the advertising listed above is within the advertising budget for the month. Some figures have not been included because exact costs cannot be determined at this time; however, the total cost for the month will not exceed the budget. Advertising is a variable cost and MSS would go with what does best. In the past, MSS has found that the ads placed in the *Daily Universe* have drawn in students and MSS would expect the same thing to happen with additional advertising in the *Daily Universe*. The radio station to be used is not specified; it would be up to the discretion of the advertiser. Radio stations frequently change their formats, so researching the station at that time of advertising is required to make sure the proper buy is made.

The giveaways will bring in additional customers who want to win the item to be given away. These items will not cost MSS too much, and at the same time they have the potential of bringing in numerous potential customers. The rules of the drawings will be: "No purchase necessary, 18 and older, must be present at the drawing, participants may enter as often as they wish, winners cannot be any employees or relatives of employees of MSS, the drawing will be held the last Friday of every month at 6 p.m., winners' names will be posted following the drawing to verify there was a drawing and a winner."

There will be a special display set up with the item to be given away as well as a box for entry slips. A free drawing for these items is a gimmick that should bring in many people who may be potential customers.

# Plan Summary

Micro Service and Sales is a profitable and successful business. Although MSS has done well in its present location, a move to the new PlumTree Shopping Center would enable MSS to grow as it should and would allow sales to increase dramatically. This is an ideal opportunity for someone who wants to own a successful business, see it grow, and make money on his investment.

MSS started under very humble circumstances of only a desk, a chair, and a phone. Under the direction of its present owner, Rob Bradford, MSS has grown into a successful and highly respected business in Orange

County. Starting with absolutely nothing, not even a computer, MSS has acquired loyal clientele in the public community as well as service agreements with local businesses and schools. MSS could become bigger and better than any computer retail outlet in Orange County and has the potential of growing into a chain that would certainly rival the larger computer stores.

MSS is set apart from the rest of the competition because it offers real service. From repairing the actual machines to giving customer support after the sale, MSS is dedicated to giving the customer the very best service. Mr. Bradford at the present time spends many hours every week just talking to potential customers and giving support to those who have bought equipment or those who have used MSS to service their system. MSS will also be different from its competition because with the proper backing, MSS will have all the popular brands of computer hardware and software and individuals will be given the opportunity to test the equipment and software before purchase.

There are numerous possibilities available to MSS, from sales and service to programming, but it needs a new location and money to make it into a better-recognized computer store of Orange County.

Micro Service and Sales has all the ingredients for a successful business except location and appropriate funds. MSS already has the reputation, the contacts, the dealerships, and the clientele. All MSS needs is a more-visible, more-easily accessible location, and appropriate funds.

## Appendixes

**Author's Note:**
*List all supporting documentation in the appendix section as noted and referenced throughout your business plan. Remember, this information should be clearly and neatly presented so the reader of your business plan can easily reference and understand the data being provided.*